CHINESE GRAMMAR
SELF TAUGHT

CHINESE GRAMMAR
SELF TAUGHT

JOHN DARROCH

Companion Volume
"CHINESE SELF TAUGHT"
By the same Author

GYAN

Published by

Gyan Publishing House
5, Ansari Road
Daryaganj, New Delhi-110002
Phone: 011-47034999, 9811692060
E-mail: books@gyanbooks.com

Distribution Network
gyanbooks.com
India, USA, Canada, UK, Australia, France

ISBN : 9788121242592 (PB)
First Published, London, 1921

2nd Impression 2020

Printed at: Gyan Press, Delhi.

Chinese Grammar
Self Taught
Author: John Darroch

Marlborough's Self-Taught Series.

Chinese Grammar Self-Taught.

BY

JOHN DARROCH, Litt.D., O.B.E.

Companion Volume:

"CHINESE SELF-TAUGHT,"

By the Author.

PRINTED IN GREAT BRITAIN.

LONDON:

E. MARLBOROUGH & Co., Ltd., 51, Old Bailey, E.C. 4.

PREFACE.

THIS volume is intended to exhibit the structure of the Chinese language in terms of grammar familiar to western readers. Chinese scholars do not study their own language by these rules. The very names we use to designate the parts of speech : nouns, verbs, &c., were unknown in China until the influx of western learning. Nevertheless, the Chinese language was a polished instrument of speech ages before that date, and Chinese scholars were as learned and, sometimes, even as pedantic as the schoolmen of the middle ages. They moulded their style on the classic examples of antiquity, and Chinese literature attains as high a standard of excellence as that of any nation ancient or modern.

Western students have neither the familiarity with the classics nor the phenomenal memories of Chinese scholars. Consequently the Chinese language often seems to them an amorphous collection of words and phrases which individually or collectively connote certain meanings, not because these ideas are inherent in the phrases used, but because custom decrees that a certain combination of words shall denote a certain meaning, but which, did custom so decree, might just as well mean something entirely different. This notion is, however, quite erroneous, and a study of the following pages will, it is hoped, convince the student that the Chinese language is as definite as our own, and so conduce to the pleasure with which he pursues the study of this most interesting tongue.

Complexities and obscurities are to be found in all languages, and Chinese has certainly a fair share of them. I have not tried to exhibit, much less to elucidate, these, but have endeavoured to show the main strong and simple lines on which the language is formed. For this reason the examples chosen to illustrate the rules given in the text are in Mandarin, the language spoken by seven-tenths of the population of China and now commonly called "pu tung hwa" (current speech). The same rules do, indeed, underlie the construction of classical Wenli, but I have preferred to use the words spoken by the common people as illustrating the language rather than the literature of China.

The student who wishes to *speak* Chinese fluently is referred to *C[illegible] Self-Taught*,* the companion volume to this, where he will find a [illegible]on on the pronunciation, romanization and tonal peculiarities of Chinese words, followed by very comprehensive vocabularies, conversational phrases and sentences, carefully selected for practical daily use and classified according to subject, with the phonetic pronunciation of the Chinese words.

I desire to record my indebtedness to R. G. Dowie, Esq., F.E.I.S., Headmaster of the Ellis Kadoorie Public School for Chinese boys in Shanghai, for efficient help in proof-reading and for many valuable suggestions in arranging the contents of this book.

J. D.

Shanghai, 1921.

---

* CHINESE SELF-TAUGHT. By J. Darroch, Litt.D., O.B.E. Cr. 8vo., in red cloth, 6/-; blue wrapper, 4/6. London: E. Marlborough & Co.

CHINESE SELF-TAUGHT AND GRAMMAR. Bound in one volume, cloth, 12/6 net.

Printed & Made in Gt. Britain by John Roberts Press Ltd., Clerkenwell Green, E.C. 1

CONTENTS.

CONTENTS.

CHINESE GRAMMAR SELF-TAUGHT

THE ORIGIN AND STRUCTURE OF THE CHINESE LANGUAGE.

It is probable—it is almost certain—that all written languages began in the same way. The cave man who made pictures on the bones of the animal he had caught in the chase and killed for food; the Indian who strips a piece of birch bark from the tree and with the burnt end of a reed from his bivouac fire makes a rude drawing of a river in the fore-ground, hills in the distance, an antelope's head, a bow and arrow, and the crescent moon and expects his squaw to understand that he has gone to the hills across the river to hunt antelope and will return when the moon wanes, are each inventing a written language. They are using symbols to represent ideas and convey a meaning from one person to another and therein lies the genesis of writing.

A glance at the pictures we have of Egyptian hieroglyphics will show us this picture language in the process of being transformed into phonetic writing. Some of the symbols are pictures of birds, beasts, or parts of the human body. These are the radicals of the hieroglyphic writing. Other symbols are conventional forms representing phonetics; these are later developments from the earlier pictograms. The Phœnician, the Greek, and other languages developed from the Egyptian, discarded the clumsy pictograms and were phonetic from the first but the ancestry of these phonetics, as of our own English script, is to be found in the picture writing on the monuments.

The earliest Chinese characters were, like the Egyptian hieroglyphics, pictures of the things signified. As, in the natural order of thought, we have first a notion of an object and think of its attributes—size, shape, colour, etc., afterwards, so, in the evolution of language common things were first represented by rude pictures and these, after they had become generally accepted as symbols of the things for which they were written, became the root words, or radicals, from which were compounded the more complicated ideographs to portray abstract ideas.

It is evident that making pictures of the things one wants to write about is a slow and clumsy way of conveying thought from one mind to another. So, from the first, efforts must have continuously been made to simplify the picture as much as was possible without destroying all resemblance to the object delineated. This process of simplification has been carried on for four thousand years until it has come to be that the Chinese characters as written now, are only symbols representing objects and ideas, their pictorial character being almost entirely obliterated. In some instances the ancient form can still be reconstructed from the modern ideograph as the following table will show.

The characters are arranged to illustrate the progressive change from the ancient to the modern form of writing.

The authority for the classification of different classes of characters is the ancient dictionary known as the 六書通 ("luh shu tung"—six forms of script). For convenience we shall follow this book in a cursory review of the growth and development of the Chinese language.

Group 1. 象形, Pictograms.

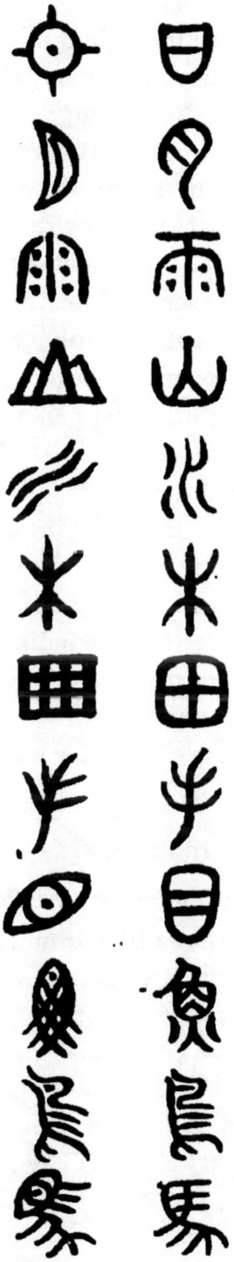

日	rïh, *the sun*
月	yüeh, *the moon*
雨	yü, *rain*
山	shan, *a hill*
水	shui, *water*
木	muh, *a tree*
田	tien, *a field*
手	shou, *the hand*
目	muh, *the eye*
魚	yü, *a fish*
鳥	niao, *a bird*
馬	ma, *a horse*

It needs no argument to prove that these and other radicals of the same class must have been amongst the first characters ever written in the Chinese language. They are all common objects. The sun and moon, the hills, trees, and rivers; these are the first things that primitive man has to do with; they are the first things he would want to speak about and when he began to write they are the first things he would want to write of. They also lend themselves to pictorial representation. One does not need to toil up the steep ascent of learning and laboriously commit to memory twenty-six phonetic signs beginning a, b, c before one can recognize a picture of the sun (note the spots on its disc; the first pen-man was an accurate observer) or the crescent moon. In adopting the pictorial script the primeval scribe was following the line of least resistance. He was in fact taking the only line that could possibly lead to success. That he chose his materials skilfully and built well and wisely is sufficiently proved by the fact that the edifice, whose foundations he laid, stands yet foursquare to every wind that blows and that after thousands of years we are still using to-day the symbols he chose when the world was young.

Group 2. 指事, "djih-szĭ," Indicators.

The second group of characters to be noted is called 指事 (djih-szī, "Indicators") and they differ from the preceding group in that, while those are pictures of things, these are pictures, or indicators, of ideas.

The numerals 1, 2, 3, etc., belong to this class. Now, it is plain that while 一 二 三 are pictorial representations of the ideas one, two, and three they are not pictures, of any one, two, or three articles. They are not pictures, for instance, of one table, two chairs, or three houses. They represent the idea signified, not the thing pictured. A moment's thought will convince us that this second class of character is a logical development of the first. It was the first, albeit, perhaps, an unconscious, step in the development of the crude picture script which was destined to become the marvellous instrument by which the most populous, and for millenniums the most highly civilized, nation on earth was to express its thought.

shang, *one thing above another*

hsia, *one thing below another*

djung, *middle*

san, *three*

szĭ, *four*

chĭh, *a foot.* The bent arm, i.e., from the elbow to the finger tips

ts'uen, *an inch.* The thumb indicating the first joint of the forefinger

ben, *a root; the origin*

moh, *the tip of a tree; the end*

yu, *right*. The right hand pointing across the body to the left

dzo, *left*. The left hand pointing across the body to the right

hwei, *to return*. A whirl pool: water that returns on its course

Note the difference in the formation of the hand radicals as written here (彐). In the preceding list it was 龵. Already we see a process of simplification at work. The radical is still further simplified when written ナ as in 左, 右 and 有. As is to be expected the hand radical is one of the commonest in the language and enters into the composition of a vast number of characters. It is possible that its different formations indicate a difference of meaning. Thus in the word 拿 na, to take, the 手 radical is written in full suggesting that the word means taking a whole handful. In 取 tsü, to choose, it is very much simplified, 又 suggesting the idea of taking between the thumb and forefinger. In 聿 yuh, a pen, still another 彐 and very common form is seen. It is scarcely possible to doubt that these different forms were originally used purposely to indicate different shades of meaning though in course of time the finer distinctions have been lost.

The first and second groups of characters are alike in one respect and dissimilar in another. They are alike in that each symbol used is a single indivisible unit. The art of combination, so common in the succeeding groups, does not enter into the construction of these characters. Each character is a picture of a well known common object and represents, in the first class, those objects themselves and, in the second class, cognate ideas suggested by the objects delineated.

In the first class a picture of the sun (☉ 日) represents the sun's disc and does not suggest light, heat, brilliancy nor any other of the abstract ideas which we might associate with the sun. In like manner the picture of a hill ( 山) represents the mass of earth we call a hill and has no connection with ideas of height or grandeur. In other words, the pictograms represent concrete objects, not abstract ideas.

In the second group, whilst the pictures are, as in the first, representations of common objects, they do not represent the objects themselves but ideas suggested by those objects.

Take, for example, the last two characters in the list given.  is a picture of a hand but it does not mean, literally, a hand but, because it is written to represent the left hand pointing to the right, it means the left hand side as distinguished from the right.

The character  囘 is a picture of swirling water in a whirlpool but its original meaning has been long forgotten by all but etymologists and it now means, to return, because the water in a whirlpool returns again and again in a gyratory motion to the place where it entered the pool.

It is so in every one of the instances given in the two lists. In the first list every character represents the object delineated and nothing else. In the second group the character never represents the object of which it is a picture but always some idea connected with and suggested by the object.

It does not need a knowledge of Chinese to realize that characters of the two classes shown above belong to the most primitive group in the language. They are all simple pictures of common objects such as would occur to untutored man in a rude age and we can well imagine the primeval penman scratching his crude pictures with a sharp flint on the slips of bamboo on which, we are told, the first Chinese characters were written.

Group 3. 會意, Indicated Meaning.

This is, perhaps, the most important of the six groups into which our authority divides the characters of which the language is composed. It will repay careful study.

ren, *benevolence.* From 人 ren, *man*, and 二 er, *two*. This character embodies the golden rule. The 二 means the other man. Do unto the other man as you would that others should do to you.

dung, *east.* From 日 rīh, *the sun*, and 木 muh, *a tree*. In the early morning the sun is seen in the east shining through the trees.

hsi, *west*. Simplified from 弓 an old form of 鳥 niao, *a bird*, and ⊗ *a nest*. The ancient form 卥 was a picture of a bird sitting on its nest. When the sun sinks in the west birds go to their nests.

wu, *military art*. From 戈 go, *a spear*, and 止 djï, *to stop*. The art by which armed aggression is stopped.

kan, *to look*. From 目 muh, *an eye* and 手 shou, *the hand*. The hand placed over the eye to shade and aid the sight.

gü, *to be afraid*. From 目 *eye*, repeated (two eyes) and 隹 djui, *birds*. A timid bird whose eyes glance right and left watching for possible enemies.

yü, *to hesitate*. From 犬 chüen, *a dog* (written as a radical) and 酋 dziu, *a chieftain*. Originally the character was the name of a kind of squirrel which had a habit of popping out of its nest and, alarmed at nothing, rushing back only immediately to repeat the performance, thus giving an admirable picture of hesitancy.

mi, *to search*. From 爪 djao, *talons*, and 見 gien, *to see*. The fingers groping for something.

ming, *clear*. From 日 *sun* and 月 *moon*, the two brightest things known.

lin, *a wood*. From 木 muh, *tree* repeated—many trees. Also 森 seng, *gloomy*, because a dense forest is dark and gloomy.

dzai, *calamity*. From 火 ho, *fire* and 巛 chwan, *water*. Fire and water are man's two deadliest enemies. To pass through fire and through water.

hsin, *truth*. From 人 ren, *man*, and 言 yen, *words*. The words of a man; something worthy of credence.

It is evident that this group of characters came into existence later than the two preceding groups. None of the characters in this class is a simple symbol; all are compounded of two or more parts. There must have been in existence a considerable number of characters belonging to the more primitive groups and these have attained currency and been in common use before the group could have been formed. Essentially it consists in the combination of two known symbols to form a third, the meaning of which will be obvious or, at least, discoverable. Remembering that these characters were devised before books were written, and that this date in China must have been at least 2000 B.C.—possibly much earlier—the student may be tempted to look behind the ideogram and speculate on the character and environment of the ancient penman who devised it. This, however, is a task beyond the powers of a learner. Sinologues even doubt whether the author of the books we follow in the interpretations given above do more than guess at the intentions of those who devised the characters. Whether these doubts are justified or not is a matter for debate. At any rate these are the interpretations of the great Chinese dictionaries on which we depend for our knowledge of the language and these dictionaries are the ultimate court of appeal in any dispute as to the meaning of any given character or phrase.

Some of the characters bear their interpretation so palpably stamped on them that it is impossible to doubt that we know what was in the mind of the original writer when he devised them and where this is not so we may safely follow the dictionary until we feel ourselves wise enough to criticise it.

Even a beginner in the study of Chinese can see that when the ancient writers began to take the known symbols and combine them to form new ones a very great stride forward was taken in the development of the language. Such new combinations are still, to a limited extent, taking place. The language is living and so manifests a natural tendency to growth.

The principle of combination was later extended to every part of the language. Two nouns are combined to form a third as in English, horse-man, window-frame, etc. Two verbs are combined to give an idea of greater force or a wider meaning than would be possible by the use of a single pictogram. These and other combinations have their root in this early discovery that by the use of two known terms you can reach out to the unknown.

Group 4. 形聲, Phonetic Symbols.

工

GUNG a workman

功 gung, *labour*
攻 gung, *to attack*
貢 gung, *tribute*
恐 kung, *to fear*
缸 gang, *a butt*
杠 gang, *a pole*
江 giang, *a river*

王

WANG a king

汪 wang, *the ocean*
枉 wang, *crooked*
旺 wang, *to flourish*
迋 wang, *to travel*
望 wang, *the full moon*

包

BAO to wrap

胞 bao, *the womb*
苞 bao, *a bud*
雹 bao, *hailstones*
飽 bao, *satisfied*
抱 bao, *to embrace*
鉋 bao, *a plane*
咆 pao, *to roar*
袍 pao, *a gown*
砲 pao, *a gun*
跑 pao, *to run*

付

FU to give

咐 fu, *to command*
附 fu, *near*
符 fu, *to match*
拊 fu, *to tap*
府 fu, *prefecture*
俯 fu, *to bow*
腑 fu, *viscera*
腐 fu, *beancurd*

This group is composed of characters of which one half—usually the right hand side—is the phonetic and the other the radical. One half suggests the meaning, the other the sound of the character. This group shows us better than any of the others how the language developed. In the natural course of evolution you have first an object, then someone invents a name for that object and, lastly, a character is invented delineating the object or, in phonetic languages, the name of the object is written and so a new word is added to the language.

Beyond doubt this group developed later in point of time than any of the others. The primitive, which gives its sound to the new character, and the radical which indicates the meaning, were already current when the need for a new word arose or the new combination could have conveyed no meaning to those who saw it for the first time.

Thus 工, *a labourer*, was probably originally a picture of the man bowed at his task. One day the need arose to speak of the man's labour apart from himself. Then the radical for strength (力) was added to differentiate labour from labourer. Tribute was paid in grain which is the product of labour and was therefore called by the same name, *gung*. Later, when the tribute began to be paid in money, the 貝 which was the original token for money was added to 工 and another new word was made.

This process is still going on. New characters are constantly being evolved. At first they are known as "unauthorized" but time impresses the hall mark of use on them and they are incorporated in the newer dictionaries and are soon as respectable as their ancestors.

From this group, too, we learn how nearly the Chinese language became phonetic. Every other language, as we have seen, began with a picture script but developed into phonetic writing. Chinese remains the only living language which retains its original pictograms. This may be a case of arrested development or, possibly, the development is still in process and about to reach its culmination in the new Dju-yin phonetic system. Time will tell, but it is certain that the progress of world thought is now impinging heavily on the Chinese written language and striking results are likely to follow.

Group 5. 轉注, Modified Meaning.

考 Kao, *old*. From this it came to mean to criticize and to examine as these were the prerogatives of the aged.

老 Lao, *aged*. Developed from the preceding character.

小 Hsiao, *small*. Two little things beside one greater, suggesting the comparatively small.

少 Shao, *few*. Developed from the preceding.

哀 Ai, *pitiful*. From 口 mouth and 衣 clothes suggesting sack-cloth and wailing.

衰 Shwai, *decaying*. Developed from the preceding.

This class is not so numerous as some of the others but it illustrates how existing characters were modified to suggest different but similar meanings; the new character retaining its likeness to the original in form and sound.

Group 6. 假借, Borrowed Meaning.

令^{1} Ling, *a command*. Read in the fourth tone 令^{4} ling, *an official*. One who commands.

長^{2} Ch'ang, *long*. Read in the third tone 長^{3} djang, *an elder*. One who has lived longer than I.

好^{3} Hao, *good*. Read in the fourth tone 好^{4} hao, *to like*, because one likes what is good.

惡^{5} Oh, *evil*. Read in the fourth tone 惡^{4} wu, *to dislike*, because one dislikes what is not good.

In this class an existing character has its tone changed and a new meaning, cognate to the old, read into it. These changes of tone are very frequent, especially in the older books. Before the language had developed to its present copiousness one character had to do the work of two. The tones were either invented to facilitate this double use or were utilized to legitimatize it.

Romanization.

The method of spelling Chinese words by means of Roman letters adopted in this book is that known as the "Standard" system. For particulars regarding that system the student is referred to Marlborough's Chinese Self-Taught, by the author, where will also be found information indispensable to a learner, regarding the tones, aspirate, pronunciation, etc., of the Chinese language which it was not possible to incorporate in this book.

Phonetic Script.

In Chinese Self-Taught it is stated that "The Chinese themselves have never represented the sounds of their characters by phonetic spelling." That statement was true when it was made but since then the Board of Education of the Chinese Government has formulated a phonetic script known as the Dju-yin dzï-mu. This script uses parts of ancient Chinese characters as phonetic symbols. These signs are the equivalents of the letters with which romanized words are spelled. To one familiar with the signs it is as easy to read the sounds of the characters in script as in Roman letters. The sound values are absolutely interchangeable. But the script is designed to teach Chinese, familiar with the formation of their own characters, to use these phonetic signs as an alphabet. It is not suitable for Western students beginning the study of Chinese. Those who learn the system of romanization used in this book will have no difficulty in learning the phonetic script should they desire to do so. A sample page of the new script is appended, not necessarily for purposes of study, but for the information of students.

Phonetic Signs of the Dju-yin System.

The phonetic alphabet contains thirty-nine sound symbols, twenty-four initials, three medials, and twelve finals. The columns are in triplicate, the phonetic symbol in the centre, the equivalent Roman letter, or letters, on the right hand side and the equivalent Chinese character on the left. In combination the symbols are written perpendicularly from the top right hand corner of the page and not horizontally as Roman letters are in an English book.

Initials 聲					母	Medials 介		母	Finals 韻		母
G	ㄍ	各	F	ㄈ	弗	I	ㄧ	衣	A	ㄚ	阿
K	ㄎ	渴	V	ㄪ	未	or yi			Ê (O)	ㄛ	惡
O	ㄫ	我	DZ	ㄗ	子	U	ㄨ	五	EH	ㄝ	也
GI	ㄐ	基	TS	ㄘ	此	or wu			EI	ㄟ	危
CHI	ㄑ	其	SZ	ㄙ	私	Ü	ㄩ	於	AI	ㄞ	愛
NI	ㄬ	尼	DJ	ㄓ	直	or yü			AO	ㄠ	嗷
D	ㄉ	得	CH	ㄔ	尺				OU	ㄡ	歐
T	ㄊ	特	SH	ㄕ	石				AN	ㄢ	安
N	ㄋ	納	H	ㄏ	合				ANG	ㄤ	昂
B	ㄅ	撥	HS	ㄒ	希				ÊN	ㄣ	恩
P	ㄆ	潑	L	ㄌ	駱				ÊNG	ㄥ	哼
M	ㄇ	末	R	ㄖ	日				ÊRH	ㄦ	兒

Double Combinations

b ㄅ i ㄧ Bi 比	t ㄊ u ㄨ Tu 土	ch ㄑ ü ㄩ Chü 去
p ㄆ u ㄨ Pu 普	n ㄋ ü ㄩ Nü 女	s ㄙ a ㄚ Sa 撒
dz ㄗ ü ㄩ Dzü 聚	g ㄍ u ㄨ Gu 古	dj ㄓ ê ㄝ Djê 者
d ㄉ i ㄧ Di 地	g ㄐ i ㄧ Gi 基	sh ㄕ ai ㄞ Shai 曬

Triple Combinations

hs ㄒ i ㄧ a ㄚ Hsia 下	d ㄉ i ㄧ ng ㄥ Ding 定	g ㄍ u ㄨ a ㄚ Gua 瓜
l ㄌ i ㄧ oh ㄛ Lioh 畧	t ㄊ u ㄨ an ㄢ Tuan 團	g ㄐ i ㄧ n ㄣ Gin 金
r ㄖ u ㄨ an ㄢ Ruan 軟	n ㄋ i ㄧ ao ㄠ Niao 鳥	ch ㄑ ü ㄩ an ㄢ Chüan 圈

The Radicals.

The radicals are, as their name suggests, the root words of the language. The student who intends to acquire a knowledge of the character must begin by learning the radicals; they are the A.B.C. of the Chinese language.

Some radicals are characters in common use; others are used, but less commonly, whilst a third class are never used except as part of some other character. The first of these three classes has been printed in large capitals, the second in small capitals and the third class is printed in ordinary type. It is suggested that the student should learn the radicals which are printed in capitals in the order indicated. The less commonly used need be learned only as occasion to use them arises.

Five Things to be Noted.

In learning the Chinese written language five things are to be noted about each character:—

(1) Its form. The *form* of ren is 人 suggesting a forked biped on two straddling legs.

(2) Its sound. The *sound* of 人 is ren, and it is the second or lower *level tone*.

(3) Its meaning. The *meaning* of 人 is *man*.

(4) Its number (if it be a radical). The *number* of the radical 人 is nine.

(5) Its alternative mode of being written (if it has any). In combination 人 is written 亻. For example, in the character 仁 ren *benevolence*, the radical 人 is written 亻.

Arrangement of Dictionary.

The characters in all Chinese dictionaries are arranged under the radicals as the words in an English dictionary are arranged under the letters of the alphabet. Some Chinese dictionaries, compiled for the use of foreigners, arrange the characters in alphabetical order, under their phonetic groups and use a key index in which the characters are classified under their radicals.

An index figure refers back to the group under which the character may be found.

In the dictionary following the series of lessons in this book the characters are arranged under their radicals as in Chinese dictionaries. This method is simpler and saves the time needed to refer from one part of the book to another. When the character is found in the index the meaning, tone, etc., are all under the eye of the student at once.

Method of Finding an Unknown Character in the Dictionary.

First, be sure the character is not itself a radical. It might be 几 gi *a stool,* the 16th radical. Or 刀 dao *a knife* the 18th. Or 至 djï *to arrive* the 133rd. Or 音 yin *a sound* the 180th. Or 香 hsiang *incense* the 186th. Or 鬼 gwei *a spirit* the 194th. All these are radicals and are only to be found under their own number in the dictionary.

Suppose the character wanted is 扣. We note that it is composed of two radicals 手 shou *a hand* and 口 kou *the mouth.* Now, the radical is placed 1st (most frequently) at the left hand side of the character. 2nd at the top. 3rd at the bottom and 4th (very seldom) at the right hand side. We therefore conclude that the character we want will be found under 手 the 64th radical. We turn to this radical in our dictionary and as the characters are arranged according to the number of strokes necessary to write them we count the number of strokes in the character—omitting the radical. We find the strokes are 丨 ㇆ 一 three in all and looking under the list of three stroke characters we find the one we are seeking and learn that its sound is *kou*, its tone, the 4th or *chü-sheng* and its meaning, *to knock*.

Or if the character wanted is 苗. We see that it is composed of two radicals 艹 grass, the 140th and 田 a field, the 102nd. In this case, as there is no radical at the left side, we surmise that we shall find the character under the radical that is on the top. We turn to the 140th radical and counting the number of strokes in 田 find them to be five. Running the eye down the list of five stroke characters we soon find the one we want and learn all that the dictionary has to tell us about it.

Again, if the unknown character were 暮. The top of this character is itself a common ideograph 莫 mo *a negative*. The radical 日 has been added to it thus making a new character out of a known phonetic. We therefore conclude that the radical, in this case, will be found at the bottom of the character and turning up the 72nd radical 日 *the sun*, we find the character we want under that key.

This method of finding a character in the dictionary may appear complicated but practice makes perfect in this, as in other operations, and we may comfort ourselves by reflecting that we are following in the footsteps of the countless scholars of China who have, for milleniums, added to their store of knowledge in this and in no other way.

RADICALS.

1 Stroke.

1.	IH	一	one ; unity.
2.	kwun	丨	a stroke.
3.	dju	丶	a point ; a period.
4.	pieh	丿	a line running obliquely to the left.
5.	ih	乙	a character in the time cycle of China.
6.	güeh	亅	a hooked end.

2 Strokes.

7.	er	二	two.
8.	tou	亠	above.
9.	REN	人亻	man.
10.	ren	儿	man.
11.	RUH	入	in, into ; to enter.
12.	BAH	八	eight.
13.	giung	冂	border waste-land.
14.	mih	冖	to cover over.
15.	bing	冫	an icicle.
16.	GI	几	a stool.
17.	kan	凵	able ; to contain.
18.	DAO	刀刂	a knife ; a sword.
19.	LIH	力	strength.
20.	bao	勹	to wrap round.
21.	bi	匕	a spoon or scoop.
22.	fang	匚	a chest.
23.	hsi	匸	to contain or conceal.
24.	SHÏH	十	ten.

25.	BUH	卜	to divine.
26.	dzieh	卩 㔾	a joint.
27.	han	厂	a ledge that shelters.
28.	szï	厶	private ; selfish.
29.	YU	又	again.

3 Strokes.

30.	KÒU	口	the mouth.
31.	wei	囗	to enclose.
32.	TŬ	土	earth.
33.	SHĪ	士	a scholar.
34.	djïh	夂	to step onwards.
35.	tsui	夊	to step slowly.
36.	HSIH	夕	evening.
37.	DA	大	great.
38.	NŬ	女	a female.
39.	DZĬ	子	a son.
40.	mien	宀	roof of a cave.
41.	TSUN	寸	an inch.
42.	HSIAO	小	little.
43.	wang	尢	bent as an ailing leg.
44.	SHĪ	尸	a corpse.
45.	che	屮	sprouting ; vegetation.
46.	SHAN	山	a hill.
47.	chwan	巛 川	streams.
48.	GUNG	工	labour.
49.	GI	己	self.
50.	GIN	巾	a napkin ; head-gear.
51.	GAN	干	a shield ; to concern.
52.	yao	幺	small.
53.	yen	广	roof of a house.

54.	yin	夂	continued motion.
55.	gung	廾	the hands folded.
56.	ih	弋	a dart.
57.	GUNG	弓	a bow.
58.	chi	彐	pointed like a pig's head.
59.	shan	彡	streaky, like hair.
60.	chĭh	彳	to step short.

4 Strokes.

61.	HSIN	心忄⺗	heart, mind.
62.	GO	戈	a lance, spear.
63.	HU	戶	a house door.
64.	SHOU	手扌	the hand.
65.	djĭh	支	a prop.
66.	puh	攴攵	to tap lightly.
67.	WEN	文	stripes; ornament; literature.
68.	DOU	斗	Chinese bushel.
69.	GIN	斤	Chinese pound; an axe.
70.	FANG	方	square.
71.	WU	无旡	not.
72.	RĬH	日	the sun; the day.
73.	YÜEH	曰	to speak.
74.	YÜEH	月	the moon.
75.	MUH	木	wood; trees.
76.	CHIEN	欠	to owe.
77.	DJĬH	止	to stop.
78.	dai	歹歺	bad.
79.	shu	殳	a quarter-staff.
80.	WU	毋	do not!

81.	BI	比	to compare; lay side by side.
82.	MAO	毛	hair, fur.
83.	chi	气	vapour.
84.	SHĪ	氏	family; name.
85.	SHUI	水 氵 氺	water.
86.	HO	火 灬	fire.
87.	djao	爪 爫	claws.
88.	FU	父	father.
89.	yao	爻	cross-wise.
90.	chiang	爿	the radical 91 reversed.
91.	pien	片	a slab of wood.
92.	YA	牙	the back teeth.
93.	NIU	牛 牜	oxen; kine.
94.	CHÜEN	犬 犭	the dog.

5 Strokes.

95.	yüen	玄	black.
96.	YÜ	玉 王	precious stones.
97.	GWA	瓜	a gourd.
98.	WA	瓦	tiles.
99.	GAN	甘	sweet.
100.	SHENG	生	to live; to produce.
101.	YUNG	用	to use.
102.	TIEN	田	fields; arable land.
103.	PIH	疋	a bale or piece of cloth, silk, etc.
104.	nih	疒	disease.
105.	boh	癶	back to back.
106	BEH	白	white.
107.	PI	皮	skin; bark.
108.	min	皿	covered dishes.

109.	MUH	目	the eye.
110.	mou	矛	a long lance.
111.	shï	矢	arrows.
112.	SHÏH	石	stone.
113.	SHÏ	示	spiritual power; revelation.
114.	rou	禸内	the print of a fox's foot.
115.	HO	禾	any kind of grain.
116.	HSÜEH	穴	a cave.
117.	LIH	立	to stand up.

6 Strokes.

118.	DJUH	竹	the bamboo
119.	MI	米	rice uncooked.
120.	SZÏ	糸	raw silk, as spun by the worm.
121.	fou	缶	earthenware.
122.	WANG	网罒	a fishing-net.
123.	YANG	羊	sheep.
124.	YÜ	羽	feathers.
125.	LAO	老	old.
126.	ER	而	and; but yet.
127.	lei	耒	the plough.
128.	ER	耳	the ear.
129.	yüh	聿	a pencil.
130.	RUH	肉⺼	flesh; meat.
131.	CHEN	臣	a statesman.
132.	DZÏ	自	self; from.
133.	DJÏ	至	to come; arrive at.
134.	giu	臼	a stone mortar.
135.	SHEH	舌	the tongue.
136.	chwan	舛	at issue; in error.

137.	DJOU	舟	ships; boats.
138.	gen	艮	limitation; character in the time cycle.
139.	SEH	色	colour.
140.	TSAO	艸艹	plants; herbs.
141.	HU	虍	the tiger.
142.	CHUNG	虫	reptiles having feet.
143.	HSÜEH	血	blood.
144.	HANG; HSING	行	*hang*, a row, *hsing*, to go, to do.
145.	I	衣	clothes.
146.	HSI	襾	the west; to cover.

7 Strokes.

147.	GIEN	見	to perceive, with the eye, nose, ear, or mind.
148.	GIOH	角	horns; a corner.
149.	YEN	言	words.
150.	GUH	谷	a valley.
151.	DOU	豆	beans.
152.	shī	豕	the pig.
153.	djai	豸	reptiles without feet.
154.	BEI	貝	a shell; precious.
155.	chih	赤	flesh colour.
156.	DZOU	走	to walk.
157.	DZUH	足	the foot; enough.
158.	SHEN	身	the body.
159.	CHÊ	車	vehicles; carts.
160.	HSIN	辛	bitter.
161.	CHEN	辰	horary period from 7 to 9 a.m.
162.	djoh	辵辶	moving and pausing.
163.	IH	邑阝	any centre of population.

164.	YU	酉	horary period, 5 to 7 p.m.
165.	PIEN	釆	to part and distinguish.
166.	LI	里	a hamlet; the Chinese mile.

8 trokes.

167.	GIN	金	the metals; gold.
168.	DJANG; CHANG	長	*djang*, to grow; *chang*, length.
169.	MEN	門	a gate, a door.
170.	fou	阜 阝	a mound of earth.
171.	dai	隶	to reach to, to arrive at.
172.	djui	隹	short-tailed birds.
173.	YÜ	雨	rain.
174.	CHING	青	sky-blue.
175.	FEI	非	negative; wrong.
176.	MIEN	面	the face; the outside.

9 Strokes.

177.	GOH	革	a hide stripped of hair.
178.	wei	韋	tanned hide.
179.	DJIU	韭	leeks.
180.	YIN	音	sound.
181.	YEH	頁	the head; page of a book.
182.	FENG	風	wind.
183.	FEI	飛	to fly as birds.
184.	SHĬH	食	to eat.
185.	SHOU	首	the head.
186.	HSIANG	香	fragrance.

10 Strokes.

187.	MA	馬	the horse.
188.	GUH	骨	bones.

189.	GAO	高	high.
190.	biao	髟	shaggy.
191.	dou	鬥	to fight; to emulate.
192.	chang	鬯	a sacrificial bowl.
193.	goh	鬲	a sacrificial vase.
194.	GWEI	鬼	spirits; demons.

11 Strokes.

195.	YÜ	魚	fish.
196.	NIAO	鳥	birds.
197.	lu	鹵	natural salts.
198.	LUH	鹿	the deer species.
199.	MEH	麥	wheat.
200.	MA	麻	hemp.

12 Strokes.

201.	HWANG	黃	yellow; clay colour.
202.	shu	黍	millet.
203.	HEH	黑	black.
204.	djïh	黹	embroidery.

13 Strokes.

205.	min	黽	the frog, or toad.
206.	ding	鼎	a two-eared tripod.
207.	GU	鼓	the drum, etc.
208.	SHU; CHU	鼠	the rat.

14 Strokes.

209.	BI	鼻	the nose.
210.	CHI	齊	arranged, in order.

15 Strokes.

211.	CHĬH	齒	front teeth.

16 Strokes.

212.	LUNG	龍	the dragon.
213.	GWEI	龜	the tortoise, turtle, etc.

17 Strokes.

214.	yoh	龠	flutes, pipes, etc.

Radicals which are written differently when used alone and in combination with other characters.

9	人 亻	94	犬 犭
18	刀 刂	96	玉 王
48	巛 川	113	示 礻
61	心 忄 ⺗	122	网 罒
64	手 扌	130	肉 月
66	攴 攵	140	艸 艹
85	水 氵	145	衣 衤
86	火 灬	163	邑 阝
87	爪 爫	170	阜 阝
93	牛 牜		

Order of Writing the Strokes.

There is a fixed order in which the strokes forming Chinese characters have to be written. Different writers do, indeed, vary slightly but the variations are within narrow limits. Generally speaking the strokes commence from the top or the left-hand side of the character. A few simple characters are appended with the various strokes written in their order from left to right.

tu *earth*	一 十 土	hsin *heart*	丶 乚 心 心
muh *wood*	一 十 才 木	hsiang *think*	木 目 心 想
kou *mouth*	丨 冂 口	rïh *sun*	冂 冃 日
tien *field*	冂 冃 用 田	yüeh *moon*	丿 月 月 月
yu *also*	㇇ 又	ming *clear*	日 月 明
yu *friend*	一 𠂇 友	nü *woman*	く 七 女
gih *lucky*	士 口 吉	dzï *son*	乛 了 子
lin *forest*	木 木 林	hao *good*	女 子 好
ko *may*	丁 口 可	er *ear*	丆 丌 冃 耳
hó *river*	氵 可 河	djï *stop*	丨 卜 卝 止
shou *hand*	丿 二 三 手	djeng *upright*	一 止 正
muh *eye*	冂 冃 月 目	an *peace*	丶 ⺀ 宀 安
kan *look*	手 目 看	na *take*	女 又 手 拏

The Chinese say that all the strokes used in the formation of their characters are found in the ideograph 永 *yung* which means eternal. If the manner in which this character is formed is noted it will furnish a key to the formation of the others. Choose a soft pen in lieu of the Chinese brush and form first the dot . Note that it is not 丶 nor 丶 but has its own slope and outline 丶. Next, write 亅 with one stroke of the pen. It is not 亅 nor 亅 but 亅; thus you have . Then again with one stroke write 乛 making . The next stroke is 丿 making the character ; lastly write 乀 and the whole character, 永, is formed.

LESSON I.

The Noun.

一[4] ih *one*	木[4] muh *tree*	老[3] lao *old*	明[2] ming *clear*	打[3] da *strike*
二[4] er *two*	林[2] lin *grove*	鳥[3] niao *birds*	山[1] shan *hill*	拉[1] la *drag*
三[1] san *three*	天[1] tien *heaven*	馬[3] ma *horse*	出[1] chuh *come out*	目[4] muh *eye*
四[4] szï *four*	地[4] di *earth*	牛[2] niu *ox*	[1]分[4] fen *divide*	看[4] kan *look*
五[3] wu *five*	人[2] ren *man*	羊[2] yang *sheep*	岔[3] cha *forked*	相[1] hsiang *mutual*
六[4] luh *six*	日[4] rïh *sun*	狗[3] gou *dog*	水[3] shui *water*	耳[3] er *ear*
七[1] tsih *seven*	月[4] yüeh *moon*	貓[2] mao *cat*	氷[1] bing *icicle*	門[2] men *door*
八[1] bah *eight*	星[1] hsing *star*	魚[2] yü *fish*	永[3] yung *eternal*	聞[2] wen *hearken*
九[3] giu *nine*	生[1] seng *life*	早[3] dzao *early*	手[3] shou *hand*	皮[2] pi *skin*
十[2] shïh *ten*	死[3] szï *death*	草[3] tsao *grass*	拜[4] bai *worship*	波[1] bo *wave*

Chinese as spoken in Peking and North China has four tones. In Southern Mandarin there are five. The small figures at the upper right hand side of the character indicate the tone. [1] is the *ping-sheng* or level tone; [2] is the *hsia-ping* or lower level tone; [3] is the *shang-sheng* or rising tone; [4] is the *chü-sheng* or departing tone. These are the four tones which are common to

North and South. The *ruh-sheng* or entering tone is not numbered but is indicated by the letter *h* at *the end* of the romanised spelling of the Chinese word. Thus the characters 一七八十 are all *ping-sheng*, the 1st tone, in the North; but as they are spelled i*h*, tsi*h*, ba*h*, shi*h*, the *h* indicates that they are *ruh-sheng* in the South.

LESSON II.

Compound Nouns.

There is no distinction between common and proper nouns in Chinese. The characters are not alphabetic and consequently cannot be distinguished by capital letters.

In the preceding pages the student has learned how the simple elementary forms of the character are compounded to represent complex or abstract ideas. In a similar manner, two separate characters are frequently joined together to form one noun containing in itself the ideas of both its components. Usually the first of the two characters is really an adjective, or descriptive noun, which merges its meaning in the substantive which it qualifies as 洋 yang, *foreign*; 人 ren, *man*; 洋 人 *a foreigner*. The following common examples are striking exceptions to this general rule; 東 tung, *east*; 西 hsi, *west*; 東 西 *things*. Why "east" and "west" combined should mean "things" may not be clear at a glance, but a moment's reflection will show that what one sees in a comprehensive gaze round the horizon from east to west is nothing more nor less than "things."

先 hsien, *before*; 生 seng, *born*; 先 生 *teacher*. The person who was born before me is, presumably, wiser than I and so is my teacher.

明 ming, *clear*; 天 tien, *a day*; 明 天 *to-morrow*. To-day is one day, then comes the dark night and after that the next clear day, or, to-morrow.

The principle underlying this custom—that of combining two separate ideas into one notion—is fundamental to the language and will be met with time and again as we proceed to analyse the various parts of speech.

Compound Nouns. Examples showing formation.

馬^{3} ma *horse*	車^{1} che *cart*	馬車 ma-che *a carriage* (*horse drawn cart*)
人^{2} ren *a man*	力^{4} lih *strength*	人力車 ren-lih-che *a man pulled cart,* *a jinricsha*
頭^{2} tou *head*	髮^{4} fah *hair*	頭髮 tou-fah *hair of the head*
手^{3} shou *hand*	套^{4} tao *a covering*	手套 shou-tao *gloves*
眼^{3} yen *eye*	睛^{1} dzing *the iris*	眼睛 yen-dzing *eyes*
眼^{3} yen *eye*	鏡^{4} ging *glass*	眼鏡 yen-ging *spectacles*
茶^{2} cha *tea*	杯^{1} bei *cup*	茶杯 cha-bei *teacup*
針^{1} djen *needle*	線^{4} hsien *thread*	針線 djen-hsien *needle-work*
書^{1} shu *book*	架^{4} gia *a frame*	書架 shu-gia *a bookcase*
木^{4} muh *wood*	匠^{4} dziang *artizan*	木匠 muh-dziang *carpenter*
鉄^{3} tieh *iron*		鉄匠 tieh-dziang *blacksmith*
鉛^{1} chien *lead*	筆^{3} bih *pencil*	鉛筆 chien-bih *lead pencil*
學^{2} hsioh *to study*	堂^{2} tang *a hall*	學堂 hsioh tang *a school*
草^{3} tsao *grass*	房^{2} fang *house*	草房 tsao-fang *thatched house*
地^{4} di *ground*	板^{3} ban *board*	地板 di-ban *flooring*
長^{2} chang *long*	褂^{4} gwa *jacket*	長褂 chang-gwa *a gown*

There are five things which the student has to learn about each Chinese character:—

1. Its sound; the sound of 地 is di (dee).
2. Its meaning; the meaning of 地 di is *earth*.
3. Its radical; the radical under which 地 di is found is 土 No. 32.
4. Its tone; the tone of 地 di is chü-sheng, fourth tone.
5. Its component parts; 地 di, is formed of 土 tu, *earth*, and 也 ye, *also*.

D.

LESSON III.

Number.

There is no sign of the plural. Whether a word is to be read in the singular or plural number is to be gathered from the context. Thus 一個人 *ih-go ren* is one *man*, but 三個人 *san-go ren*, is three *men*. There is no change in writing the character 人 "man," but the change of number is sufficiently evident by the use of 一 *one*, or 三 *three*, before the noun.

五個洋人 wu-go yang ren ; *five foreigners.*

八個女人 bah-go nü ren ; *eight women.*

十個學堂 shïh-go hsioh-tang ; *ten schools.*

十三個鳥 shïh-san go niao ; *thirteen birds.*

十六個東西 shïh-luh go dung-hsi ; *sixteen things.*

二十塊洋錢 er-shïh kwai yang chien ; *twenty dollars.*

三十一個茶盃子 san-shïh-ih go cha-bei-dzï ; *thirty-one tea cups.*

九十五個房子 giu-shïh-wu go fang-dzï ; *ninety-five houses.*

二百二十三個人 er-beh er-shïh san go ren ; *two hundred and twenty-three men.*

From eleven to nineteen the numerals are formed by adding the digits after ten as 十二 shïh-er ; *twelve.* 十三 shïh-san ; *thirteen.* etc.

The digits are added in like manner after twenty, thirty, etc., as 二十二 er-shïh-er ; *twenty-two.* 三十三 san-shïh-san ; *thirty-three.* etc.

We say in English "A hundred and one." The "and" is expressed after hundreds by the character 零 ling. Thus 二百零一 er-beh ling ih ; *two hundred and one.* 二百零二 er-beh ling er ; *two hundred and two.*

Ling is not used after decimals, only after hundreds or thousands.

個 Go, *each*, is a numerary adjunct—its meaning and function will be further elucidated in a later lesson.

The numerary adjunct (sometimes called a "classifier") comes between the number and the noun. As above 一 個 人 ih go reu, *one piece man*. The invariable order is first the number then the adjunct and the noun last.

子[3] dzï, *son*, is used as an enclitic and, as such, has no meaning.

In South and Central China it is added to almost every noun in common speech.

兒[3] er, *a son*, is always 兒 子 er-dzï;
驢[2] lü, *a donkey*, is always 驢 子 lü-dzi;
桌 djoh, *a table*, is always 桌 子 djoh-dzï; etc.

LESSON IV.

這[4] dje *this*

那[4] na *that*

這[4]個[4] dje-go *this*

那[4]個[4] na-go *that*

裏[3] li *inside*

這[4]些[1] dje-hsie *these*

這[4]裏[3] dje-li *here*

那些 na-hsie *those*

那[4]裏[3] na-li *there*

是[4] shï *is*

不[4] buh *not*

有[3] yu *have*

要[4] yao *want*

來[2] lai *come*

沒[2] muh *lost*

沒[2]有[3] muh-yu *have not*

先[4] hsien *before*

先[4]生[1] hsien-seng *a teacher*

孩[2]子[3] hai-dzï *a child*

學[2]生[1] hsioh-seng *a scholar*

銅[2] tung *brass*

錢[2] chien *money*

洋[2]錢[2] yang-chien *dollars*

銅[2]錢[2] tung-chien *cash*

百[3] beh *hundred*

千[1] chien *thousand*

萬[4] wan *myriad*, *ten thousand*

NOTE:—Shï 是 is the commonest verb in the language. Verbs, like nouns, do not distinguish the plural, hence shï 是 is either "is" or "are" as the sentence demands.

Gender.

Gender is indicated by prefixing to the noun the character for "male" or "female" and this character qualifies the substantive just as an adjective does.

男[2] nan, *male* 女[3] nü, *female.*

一個男人 ih-go nan ren; *one man.*

三個女人 san-go nü ren; *three women.*

五個男孩子 wu-go nan hai-dzï; *five boys.*

十六個女孩子 shïh-luh go nü hai-dzï; *sixteen girls.*

一百零三個男學生 ih-beh ling san go nan hsioh-seng; *one hundred and three boy scholars.*

二百五十四個女學生 er-beh wu-shïh-szï go nü hsioh-seng; *two hundred and fifty-four girl scholars.*

一個女先生 ih-go nü hsien-seng; *one lady teacher.*

多[1] do *many*

少[3] shao *few*

多[1]少[3] do-shao *how many*

大[4] da *great*

小[3] hsiao *small*

前[2] chien *before*

後[4] hou *after*

能[2] neng *ability*

做[1] dzo *to do*

外[4] wai *outside*

事[4] szï *a matter*

子[3] dzï *a son* (an enclitic)

字[4] dzï *a character*

樣[4] yang *a kind*

一[1]樣[4] ih-yang (*one kind*) *the same*

不[4]一[1]樣[4] buh ih yang *not the same*

是[4]一[1]樣[4] shïh ih yang *it is the same*

不[4]是[4]一[1]樣[4] buh shïh ih yang *it is not the same*

LESSON V.

The Pronouns.

The pronouns in Mandarin are

我 o, *I*, or *me*.	我們 o-men, *we*, or *us*.
你 ni, *thou*.	你們 ni-men, *you*.
他 ta, *he*, *she* or *him*.	他們 ta-men, *they*, or *them*.

們 men, is the sign of the plural.

There is no neuter pronoun: the third person singular 他 ta, is sometimes used for "it."

The Possessive.

The possessive case is indicated by the particle 的 dih (and dy) which is affixed to a noun or pronoun as the apostrophe is in English.

我的 o-dy, *my*. 你的 ni-dy, *thine*. 他的 ta-dy, *his*.

我們的 o-men dy; *ours*.
你們的 ni-men dy; *yours*.
他們的 ta-men dy; *theirs*.
我的東西 o-dy dung-hsi; *my things*.
他們的書 ta-men dy shu; *their books*.
學生的鉛筆 hsioh-seng dy chien-bih; *the scholar's lead pencil*.
先生的書架 hsien-seng dy shu-gia; *the teacher's book case*.
這是你的三十塊錢 dje shï ni-dy san-shïh kwai chien; *this is your thirty dollars*.
他們是女先生的學生 ta-men shï nü hsien-seng dy hsioh-seng; *they are the lady teacher's scholars*.
大孩子是我的小孩子是你的 da hai-dzi shï o-dy; hsiao hai-dzï shï ni-dy; *the big child is mine; the small child is yours*.

這個馬是他的那個車子是先生的 dje-go ma shï ta-dy; na-go che-dzï shï hsien seng dy; *this horse is his; that cart is the teacher's.*

你有多少錢 ni yu do-shao chien, *how much money have you?*

NOTE:—之 djï is the sign of the possessive in the wen-li or classic style.

LESSON VI.

The Adjective.

In Chinese, as in English, the adjective is used to qualify the noun directly or as a complement of a verb. In the first case the adjective precedes the noun; in the second it follows the verb.

Preceding the noun.

好人 hao ren; *good man.*

大魚 da yü; *big fish.*

小錢 hsiao chien; *small cash.*

老馬 lao ma; *old horse.*

Following the verb.

那個人是好 na-go ren shï hao; *that man is good.*

這個魚是大 dje-go yü shï da; *this fish is big.*

你的錢是小 ni-dy chien shï hsiao; *your cash is small.*

The verb (是 shï) is commonly omitted and understood in assertive sentences as :—

先生的學生多 hsien-seng dy hsioh-seng do; *the teacher's scholars (are) many.*

那個人的馬好 na-go ren dy ma hao; *that man's horse (is) good.*

他們的孩子多 ta-men dy hai-dzï do; *their children (are) numerous.*

木匠的木頭長 muh-djiang dy muh-tou chang; *the carpenter's wood (is) long.*

今天好的多 gin tien hao dy do; *to-day (is) much better.*

這個好的不少 che-go hao dy puh shao; *this (is) much better*

List of Adjectives.

貴^4 guei *honorable*	狹^2 hsiah *narrow*	兇^1 hsiung *fierce*	淸^1 ching *clear*
賤^4 gien *mean*	冷^3 leng *cold*	能^2 neng *able*	濁^2 djoh *dirty*
厚^4 hou *thick*	熱^4 reh *hot*	苦^3 ku *bitter*	輕^1 ching *light*
薄^2 boh *thin*	生^1 seng *raw*	忙^2 mang *busy*	重^4 djung *heavy*
高^1 gao *high*	熟^2 shuh *cooked*	閒^2 hsien *leisure*	爽^3 shwang *lively*
低^1 di *low*	明^2 ming *clear*	便^4 bien *convenient*	困^4 kun *weary*
粗^1 tsu *coarse*	暗^4 an *dark*	聾^2 lung *deaf*	緊^3 gin *tight*
細^4 hsi *fine*	長^2 chang *long*	遠^3 yüen *distant*	鬆^1 sung *loose*
黑^4 heh *black*	短^3 dwan *short*	近^4 gin *near*	急^2 gih *hurried*
白^2 beh *white*	早^3 dzao *early*	空^1 kung *empty*	疼^2 teng *painful*
美^3 mei *beautiful*	晚^3 wan *late*	鮮^1 hsien *fresh*	方^1 fang *square*
醜^3 chou *ugly*	遲^2 chï *slow*	新^1 hsin *new*	圓^2 yüen *circular*
老^3 lao *old*	速^4 shuh *fast*	舊^4 giu *old*	團^2 twan *globular*
幼^4 yu *young*	眞^1 djen *true*	貧^2 pin *poor*	扁^3 bien *flat*
快^4 kuai *quick*	假^3 gia *false*	富^4 fu *rich*	怒^4 nu *angry*
慢^4 man *slow*	正^4 djeng *upright*	硬^4 ying *hard*	惱^3 nao *annoyed*
鈍^4 dun *blunt*	歪^1 wai *deflected*	軟^3 rwan *soft*	喜^3 hsi *pleased*
利^4 li *sharp*	直^2 djïh *straight*	餓^4 o *hungry*	歡^1 hwan *joyful*
廣^3 guang *broad*	彎^1 wan *crooked*	飽^3 pao *satiated*	甜^2 tien *sweet*
窄^4 dzeh *narrow*	嫩^4 nwen *tender*	渴^3 koh *thirsty*	完^2 wan *finished*
寬^1 kwan *wide*	良^2 liang *good*	足^4 dzuh *satisfied*	全^2 tsüen *perfect*

LESSON VII.

The Adjective.

The Comparative is formed by adding 些[1] hsie *a little*, 一[4]點[3] ih dien *an iota*, 多[1] do *many*, or 不[4]少[3] buh shao *not few*, to the adjective. Note that the comparative follows the adjective and does not precede it as in English.

那個人好些 na-go ren hao hsie; *that man is better* (*than some other*).

這個房子大些 dje-go fang-dzï da hsie; *this house is bigger*.

我們的錢多些 o-men dy chien do-hsie; *our money is more* (*than theirs*).

一天好一點 ih tien hao ih dien; *each day is a little better*.

你的馬好一點 ni dy ma hao ih dien; *your horse is a little better* (*than mine*).

The words 比 bi, *to compare* or 較 giao, *to compare*, placed before the object strengthens the comparison.

那個人的東西比這個人的東西好些 na-go ren dy dung-hsi bi dje-go ren dy dung-hsi hao hsie; *that man's goods are better than this man's*.

你們的學堂比我們的大一點 ni-men dy hsioh-tang bi o-men dy da ih dien; *your school is a little larger than ours*.

他比我能些 ta bi o neng hsie; *he is more able than I*.

好人比不好人較少 hao ren bi buh hao ren giao shao; *good men are fewer than bad man*.

這個車子較那個車子重些 dje-go che-dzï giao na-go che-dzï djung hsie; *this barrow is heavier than that one*.

外國狗比中國的狗兇些 wai-gwoh gou bi djung-gwoh dy gou hsiung-hsie; *foreign dogs are fiercer than Chinese dogs*.

The student should note the compound structure of the comparative. 比 bi,..............好 hao, is really the same as the English phrase "*better than.*" The 比 bi, takes the place of "*than*" and 好 hao, that of "*better*"; but instead of saying as in English "He is better than I" Chinese idiom runs 他比我好 "*he than I better* (*is*)." This is a very common construction and is comparable to that of co-ordinate conjunctions such as either.........or, though............yet, in English. It will be met with again in the lessons on Verbs and Prepositions.

Compound Adjectives. We have seen that two common nouns combine to form a compound noun. Adjectives—and, indeed, all the parts of speech—are also single and compound. The single adjectives, that constitute the combination, are frequently of different and, sometimes, of apparently incongruous meanings. Yet the compound adjective, formed from their combination, is often remarkably apposite and is always forceful. The singular facility with which the units, of which the language is formed, combine to form new and striking words is one of the most notable features of Chinese and adds much to its flexibility and beauty.

富[4] fu *wealthy*
貴[4] gwei *honorable*
富貴 fu-gwei *rich*

歡[1] huan *joy*
喜[3] hsi *pleasure*
歡喜 huan-hsi *pleased*

貧[2] pin *poor*
窮[2] chiung *impoverished*
貧窮 pin-chiung *poor*

小[3] hsiao *small*
心[1] hsin *heart*
小心 hsiao-hsin *careful*

冷[3] leng *cold*
熱[4] reh *hot*
冷熱 leng-reh *temperature*

大[4] da *great*
意[4] *i* *thought*
大意 da-i *careless*

寬[1] kwan *wide*
綽[1] choh *large*
寬綽 kwan-choh *spacious*

完[2] wan *finished*
全[2] tsüen *completely*
完全 wan-tsüen *perfect*

潔[2] gieh
white silk

淨[4] dzing
clear

潔淨 gieh-dzing
pure

乾[1] gan
dry

淨[4] dzing
pure

乾淨 gan-dzing
clean

光[1] gwang
light

亮[4] liang
bright

光亮 gwang-liang
bright

舒[1] shu
relaxed

服[4] fuh
yielding

舒服 shu-fuh
comfortable

懶[3] lan
lazy

惰[4] do
indolent

懶惰 lan-do
lazy

熱[2] reh
hot

心[1] hsin
heart

熱心 reh-hsin
zealous

便[4] bien
convenient

當[1] dang
fitting

便當 bien-dang
convenient

四[4] szï
four

方[1] fang
square

四方 szï-fang
four-square

憂[1] yu
anxiety

愁[2] tsou
sorrow

憂愁 yu-tsou
sorrowful

伶[2] ling
active

俐[4] li
sharp

伶俐 ling-li
clever

奇[2] chi
strange

怪[4] gwai
uncanny

奇怪 chi-gwai
marvellous

儉[3] gien
thrifty

省[3] seng
sparing

儉省 gien-seng
economical

能[2] neng
ability

幹[4] gan
managing

能幹 neng-gan
able

爽[3] shwang
lively

快[4] kwai
quick

爽快 shwang-kwai
frolicsome

便[2] bien *cheap*
宜[2] i *proper*
便 宜 pien-i *cheap*

危[2] wei *a defile*
險[3] hsien *a limit*
危 險 wei-hsien *dangerous*

新[1] hsin *new*
鮮[1] hsien *fresh*
新 鮮 hsin-hsien *fresh*

公[1] gung *public*
道[4] dao *justice*
公 道 gung-dao *just*

許[3] hsü *excess*
多[1] do *many*
許 多 hsü-do *many*

疼[2] teng *painful*
愛[4] ai *love*
疼 愛 teng-ai *loving*

污[1] wu *dirty*
穢[4] hwei *weeds*
污 穢 wu-hwei *filthy*

要[4] yao *to want*
緊[3] gin *tight*
要 緊 yao-gin *important*

緊[3] gin *tight*
急[2] gih *haste*
緊 急 gin-gih *urgent*

客[4] keh *a guest*
氣[4] chi *breath*
客 氣 keh-chi *polite*

驕[3] giao *haughty*
傲[4] ao *stubborn*
驕 傲 giao-ao *proud*

黑[4] heh *black*
暗[4] an *dark*
黑 暗 heh-an *dark*

軟[3] rwan *a wobbly cart*
弱[4] roh *a broken bow*
軟 弱 rwan-roh *weak*

老[3] lao *old*
實[4] shïh *true*
老 實 lao-shïh *honest*

快^{4} kwai *quick*

活^{2} hoh *lively*

快 活 kwai-hoh *happy*

團^{2} twan *a lump*

圓^{2} yüen *circular*

團 圓 twan-yüen *round*

惱^{3} nao *irritate*

怒^{4} nu *anger*

惱 怒 nao-nu *angry*

平^{2} ping *level*

安^{1} an *quiet*

平 安 ping an *peaceful*

蠢^{3} chwen *an insect*

笨^{4} ben *bamboo*

蠢 笨 chwen-ben *stupid*

聰^{1} tsung *acute hearing*

明^{2} ming *clear sight*

聰 明 tsung-ming *wise*

節^{2} gieh *a section*

制^{4} djï *to regulate*

節 制 gieh-djï *temperate*

健^{4} gien *strong*

壯^{4} djwang *big*

健 壯 gien-djwang *robust*

LESSON VIII.

The Adjective.

The superlative is formed by prefixing one of the following adverbs to the adjective 頂 ding, *the top*, 最 dzui, *very*, 甚 shen, *very*, 太 tai, *very*, 很 hen, *exceedingly*, *very*.

你的褂子頂長 ni dy gwa-dzï ding chang; *your gown is very long.*

那個人最好 na-go ren dzui hao; *that man is very good.*

中國人的銅錢甚多 djung-gwoh ren dy tung chien shen do; *Chinese have plenty of cash.*

外國人的洋錢太多 wai gwoh ren dy yang chien tai do; *foreigners have too many dollars.*

很 hen, *very*, used alone, precedes the adjective as do the other adverbs.

你妹妹的頭髮很長 ni mei-mei dy tou-fah hen chang; *your sister's hair is very long.*

這個老驢子很好 dje-go lao lü-dzï hen hao; *this old donkey is very good.*

When 很 hen, *exceedingly*, is preceded by the verb 得 deh, *to obtain*, it follows the verb and, though placed at the end of the sentence, has a reflex action and qualifies the preceding adjective in an intensitive sense.

這個藥苦得很 dje-go yoh ku deh-hen; *this medicine is very bitter.*

你那個鳥好得很 ni na-go niao hao deh-hen; *that bird of yours is very good.*

我父親的馬車快得很 o fu-chin di ma-che kwai deh-hen; *my father's carriage is very swift.*

你女兒的針線好得很 ni nü-er dy djen-hsien hao deh-hen; *your daughter's needle-work is very good.*

NOTE:—When a pronoun in the possessive case is followed by a noun in the possessive case the possessive particle 的 dy, is, for the sake of euphony, omitted after the pronoun. In accordance with this rule the sentence "My father's carriage" is not 我的父親的馬車 "o-*dy* fu-chin *dy* ma-che," but 我父親的馬車 "o fu-chin *dy* ma-che" and "your daughter's needle-work" is not 你的女兒的針線 "nee-*dy* nü-er *dy* djen-hsien but 你女兒的針線 ni nü-er *dy* djen-hsien. In other words, the possessive particle does not occur twice in a short sentence.

The adverb 極 gih, *extremely*, is remarkable in that it may precede or follow its adjective. It has the same meaning in either position; but in the latter case it is probably an ellipsis for the adverbial phrase 到 極 點 dao gih dien, *to the extreme point.*

這個事極好 dje-go szï gih hao; *this affair is most gratifying.*

小學生壞極 hsiao hsioh-seng hwai gih; *the little scholars are very naughty.*

NOTE:—(1) 極 gih, is scarcely used colloquially except to qualify the adjectives 好 hao, *good*, and 壞 hwai, *bad*.

(2) Note the absence of the verb from the above sentences. See rule page 38.

還 hwan (also commonly read hai), *to repay*, *to return*.

This character is peculiar in that, originally a verb, it is used as an adverb and modifies the adjective 好 hao, *good*, IN A NEGATIVE SENSE.

他的話好 ta dy hwa hao; *his words were good.*

他的話還好 ta dy hwa hai hao; *his words were fairly good.*

這個書還好 dje-go shu hai hao; *this book is fairly good.*

The affirmation is still further modified when the adjective is repeated with the modifying word between.

他的話好還好 ta dy hwa hao hai hao; *his words were only fairly good*

這個書好還好 dje-go shu hao hai hao; *this book is not very good.*

It is to be noted that 還 hai has an intensative sense when used with any word except 好 hao, *good*.

他比你還壞 ta bi ni hai hwai; *he is even worse than you.*

我父親的錢比他的還多些 o fu-chin dy chien bi ta dy hai do hsie; *my father's money is even more than his.*

外國比中國還大 wai gwoh bi djung-gwoh hai da; *foreigndom is even larger than China.*

LESSON IX.

Distributive Adjectives.

These are 各 goh, 每 mei, 個 go, and 諸 dju. Each of these characters means *each*, *every*, *all*, *every one*, etc. There are shades of distinction in their use but practice will indicate this better than any rule. They invariably precede the noun.

個 go, *each*, we have had frequently as a classifier.

一個人 ih-go ren; *one man.*

三個馬 san-go ma; *three horses.*

個人 go ren; *each, individual.*

個個人 go go ren; *each single individual.*

一個一個的 ih-go ih-go dy; *one by one.*

一個一個的說話 ih-go ih-go dy shwoh hwa; *speak one by one.*

各 goh, is the commonest word for "*each.*"

各人 goh ren; *each man.* **各事** goh szī; *each affair.*

各地方 goh di-fang; *each place.*

各有各見 goh yu goh gien; *each has his own viewpoint.*

每 mei, *each*, has reference to time.

每日 mei rïh; *each day.*

每一個禮拜 mei ih-go li-bai; *each week.*

每禮拜三日 mei li-bai san rïh; *every Wednesday.*

諸 dju, has the sense of "*each and all.*"

諸人 dju ren; *each man.*

諸位 dju wei; *each honourable person* (this is the polite and proper way to address a number of people).

諸位弟兄 dju wei di-hsiung; *each of you brethren.*

Words Meaning All.

凡 fan, *all*, and **衆** djung, *all*, precede the noun.

凡事 fan szī; *all affairs.* **凡人** fan ren; *all men.*

衆位 djung wei; *all of you.*

衆生 djung seng; *all living (people).*

衆口如一 djung kou ru ih; *all with one voice.*

衆 djung, the original meaning of **衆** djung is *a crowd:* properly it should be used to qualify nouns that refer only to living beings.

萬 wan, 10,000 is also an adjective meaning *all*.

萬國 wan gwoh ; *all countries*.

萬人 wan ren ; *all men*.

萬物 wan wuh ; *all things*.

一切 ih chieh ; *all*.

攏總 lung-dzung ; *all*.

NOTE:—The knife radical in 切 chieh. Properly, though not necessarily, chieh, means *all*, in the sense of the whole slice ; *a homogeneous whole*.

攏 lung, has the hand radical and its etymology suggests *an armful*.

總 dzung, is the *large rope* that draws the net together.

攏總 lung-dzung, means *the whole armful* or, *all the fish*, good and bad, in the net : *a heterogeneous whole*.

These two compound adjectives precede and qualify the substantive but they require the possessive particle 的 dy, to connect them with the noun. They thus form adjective phrases and 的 dy, in this connection, is the adjectival particle.

這一切的話你們都聽見 dje ih-chieh dy hwa ni-men du ting-gien ; *you have heard all these words*.

一切的事都辦完了 ih-chieh dy szï du ban wan-liao ; *everything has been attended to*.

攏總的人來到了 lung-dzung dy ren lai dao-liao ; *all the men have arrived*.

攏總的東西都收拾起來了 lung-dzung dy dung-hsi du shou-shïh chi-lai-liao ; *all the things have been gathered up*.

ADVERBS are to be distinguished from adjectives.

In translating a Chinese sentence into English the order of the words is, necessarily, transposed. Though that translation is accurate which correctly renders the sense of the Chinese in English the student must not translate the Chinese sentence into English and then parse the English translation. The Chinese sentence itself is to be analysed. The following examples will illustrate this principle.

皆 giai, *all.* 都 du, *all* and 全 tsüen, *altogether,* all precede and modify the verb as 凡 fan, *all.* 衆 djung, *all* and 萬 wan, *a myriad* precede and qualify the noun. The first three characters 皆 giai, 都 du, and 全 tsüen, are adverbs. 凡 fan, 衆 djung, and 萬 wan, are adjectives.

萬人都有愛國心 wan ren du yu ai gwoh hsin; *all men love their country.*

衆生皆知孝敬父母 djung seng giai djï hsiao-ging fu-mu; *all men know (how) to love their parents.*

凡事全要預備停當 fan szï tsüen yao yü-bei ting-dang; *everything must be prepared perfectly.*

The English translations of these Chinese sentences express the meaning accurately but do not exhibit the structure of the Chinese; this is impossible in idiomatic English but note that, in the first sentence, the noun 人 ren, is preceded and qualified by the adjective 萬 wan. In like manner the verb 有 yu, is preceded and modified by the adverb 都 du. The sentence might be rendered "*All men invariably have a love-their-country heart.*"

In the second sentence the noun 生 seng, is preceded and qualified by the adjective 衆 djung. The verb 知 djï, is preceded and modified by the adverb 皆 giai. The sentence might be translated "*All living (people) universally know to love their parents.*"

In the third sentence the noun 事 szï, is preceded and qualified by the adjective 凡 fan. The verb 要 yao, is preceded and modified by the adverb 全 tsüen. We might translate "*Everything absolutely must be prepared perfectly.*"

人人皆有德 ren ren giai yu deh; *every man has (some) virtue.*

In the English translation the words "*every man*" are the equivalent of 人人 ren ren. 皆 giai is not translated and the pronoun "it" is added to make the sentence conform to English idiom. The sentence if translated literally would read "*All men uniformly have virtue.*" The word "*uniformly*" exactly reproducing the force of the adverb 皆 giai.

學生皆有書 hsioh-seng giai yu shu; *every scholar has a book.*

外國人都是這個樣子 wai-gwoh ren du shĭ dje-go yang-dzĭ; *foreigners are all like this.*

個個都是如此 go go du shĭ ru tzĭ; *every one is like this.*

這些東西我全不要 dje-hsie dung-hsi o tsüen buh yao; *I don't want any of those things.*

他的病全愈了 ta dy bing tsüen yü liao; *his sickness is completely cured.*

Each of the above Chinese sentences contains an adverb but he adverb is not expressed in the English translation except in the last sentence; nevertheless, its position and function in Chinese should be carefully noted.

父^4 fu *father*

母^3 mu *mother*

親^1 chin *attached to, loved*

戚^4 chih *relatives*

父^{4}母^3 fu-mu *parents*

父^{4}親^1 fu-chin *father*

母^{3}親^1 mu-chin *mother*

親^{1}戚^4 chin-chih *relatives*

女^{3}兒^2 nü-er *daughter*

兒^{2}女^3 er-nü *family, children*

兄^{1}弟^4 hsiung-di *younger brother*

弟^{4}兄^1 di-hsiung *brethren*

哥^{1}哥^1 go-go *elder brother*

妹^{4}妹^4 mei-mei *younger sister*

姐^{3}姐^3 dzie-dzie *elder sister*

姊^{3}妹^4 dzĭ-mei *sisters*

中^1 djung *middle*

飯^4 fan *food*

藥^4 yoh *medicine*

情^2 ching *feelings*

事^{4}情^2 szĭ-ching *affairs*

今^1 gin *now*

今^{1}天^1 gin-tien *to-day*

房^{2}子^3 fang-dzĭ *a house*

房^{2}屋^1 fang-wuh *a house*

地^{4}方^1 di-fang *a place*

放^4 fang *to let go*

話^4 hwa *words*

說^1 shwoh *to speak*

說^{1}話^4 shwoh-hwa *to speak*

朋^{2}友^3 peng-yu *a friend*

命^4 ming *fate, life*

生^{1}命^4 seng-ming *life* (human)

鹽^2 yen *salt*

糖$^?$ tang *sugar*

饅^{2}頭^2 man-tou *native loaf*

麵^{4}包^1 mien-bao *foreign loaf*

肉^4 ruh *flesh*

牛^{2}肉^4 niu-ruh *beef*

豬^1 dju *a pig*

豬^{1}肉^4 dju-ruh *pork*

羊^{2}肉^4 yang-ruh *mutton*

國^2 gwoh *kingdom*

中^{1}國^2 djung-gwoh *China*

外^4 wai *outside*

外^{4}國^2 wai-gwoh *outside countries; foreigndom*

內^4 nei *inside*

重^4 djung *heavy*

輕^1 ching *light*

LESSON X.

Reflexive Pronouns.

The use of the personal pronouns has already been explained. See page 37. The Reflexive pronouns are formed by adding 自己 dzi-gi, *self*, to the personal pronouns.

我^{3}自^{4}己^3 o dzï-gi *myself.*

你^{3}自^{4}己^3 ni dzï-gi *thyself.*

他^{1}自^{4}己^3 ta dzï-gi *himself.*

我^{3}自^{4}己^{3}看^{1}見^4 o dzï-gi kan-gien *I saw it myself.*

你^{3}自^{4}己^{3}聽^{1}見^4 ni dzï-gi ting-gien *you heard it yourself.*

他^{1}自^{4}己^{3}如^{2}此^{2}說^1 ta dzï-gi ru-tzï shwoh; *he himself spoke thus.*

Possessive.

On the use of the possessive particle 的 dih or dy, see p. 37.

這是我自己的書 dje shï o dzï-gi dy shu; *this is my own book.*

攏總的東西都是你自己的 lung-dzung dy dung-hsi du shï ni dzï-gi dy; *all the things are your own.*

這是他自己的孩子 dje shï ta dzï-gi dy hai-dzï; *this is his own child.*

There is no plural of 自己 dzï-gi: though sometimes one hears a sentence like 他們自己的 ta-men dzï-gi dy; *their very own.* Such a sentence is inelegant as dzï-gi, *self* is a pronoun in the singular number.

聽[1] ting
to listen.

見[4] gien
to perceive.

看 kan
to look.

看[1]見[4] kan-gien
to look and see.

聽[1]見[4] ting-gien
to hear.

回[2] hwei
to return; a time.

應[1] ying
right; ought.

當[1] dang
fitting; ought.

應[1]當[1] ying-dang
ought.

如[2] ru
like.

此[3] tsï
this.

如[2]此[3] ru-tzï
thus.

經[1] ging
a line; a book.

五[3]經[1] wu ging
the five classics.

聖[4] sheng
a sage; holy.

聖[4]經[1] sheng-ging
the Bible.

已[3] i
finished.

已[3]經[1] i-ging
already.

禮[3] li
propriety.

拜[4] bai
to salute.

禮[3]拜[4] li-bai, *worship;* and *a week* since Sunday, the worship day, comes once in seven days.

各人有他應當做的事 goh ren yu ta ying-dang dzo dy szï; *each man has his own proper work.*

諸位不要如此說 dju-wei buh yao ru-tzï shwoh; *please, gentlemen, do not speak thus.*

他每回來都是這個樣子 ta mei hwei lai du shï dje-go yang-dzï; *every time he comes it is always like this.*

禮拜日應當看聖書 li-bai rïh ying-dang kan sheng shu; *on Sunday we ought to read the Bible.*

一切的東西皆是我的 i-chieh dy dung-hsi giai shï o dy; *all the things are mine.*

攏總的東西都是你的 lung-dzung dy dung-hsi du shï ni-dy; *all the things are yours.*

我已經看見他 o i-ging kan-gien ta; *I have already seen him.*

The days of the week are usually named

禮拜一 li-bai ih *Monday.*

禮拜二 li-bai er *Tuesday.*

禮拜三 li-bai san *Wednesday.*

禮拜四 li-bai szï *Thursday.*

禮拜五 li-bai wu *Friday.*

禮拜六 li-bai luh *Saturday.*

禮拜日 li-bai rïh *Sunday.*

The Japanese term for week is 星期 hsing-chi, *star period.* They use this term because the days of the week are named after certain stars. The terms 星期一 hsing-chi ih, 星期二 hsing-chi-er, for Monday, Tuesday, etc., are common in China.

Demonstrative Pronouns.

這^{4}個^4 dje-go *this.*

這^{4}些^4 dje-hsie *these.*

那^{4}個^3 na-go *that.*

那^{4}些^3 na-hsie *those.*

We have already had dje-go and na-go as demonstrative adjectives: as in English the words are used in both senses but most frequently as adjectives.

這個褂子是黑的那個是白的 dje-go gwa-dzï shï heh-dy na go shï beh-dy ; *this gown is black ; that is white.*

這個學生好那個不好 dje-go hsioh-seng hao, na-go buh hao ; *this scholar is good ; that one is bad.*

The plural is uncommon though one might say :—

這些東西好那些不好 dje-hsie dung-hsi hao ; na-hsie buh hao ; *these things are good ; those are bad.*

LESSON XI.

Interrogatives.

There are three common interrogatives. They are 嗎 ma, 麽 mo, and, 呢 ni. These are placed, like our point of interrogation, at the end of the sentence and fulfil the same purpose, but whereas, in English, the point of interrogation is a sign only these are words and are pronounced as are the other words in the sentence.

你[3]看[1]見[4]他[1]嗎[1] ni kan gien ta ma
have you seen him?

你[3]聽[1]見[4]這[4]個[4]話[4]呢[1] ni ting gien dje-go hua ni
do you hear these words?

這[4]是[4]你[3]作[4]的[4]麽[1] dje shï ni dzoh dy mo
did you do this?

Note that, in Chinese, a question is asked by postulating a statement and appending the interrogative.

Statement 你[3]看[1]見[4]他[1] ni kan gien ta.
you have seen him.

Interrogative 嗎[1] ma?
have you?

就[4] dziu
thereupon.

就[4]是[4] dziu shï
even so, etc.

意[4] i
meaning, thought.

思[1] szï
to think.

意[4]思[1] i-szï
meaning.

想[3] hsiang
reflect.

思[1]想[3] szï hsiang
reflect on.

何[2] ho
how, why.

如[2] ru
like.

何[2]如[2] ho ru
how much better.

何[2]嘗[2] ho chang
when?

同[2] tung
together.

如[2]同 *like, as.*

因[1] yin
because, for.

爲[2] wei
to be.

因[1]爲[4] yin wei
because.

緣[2]故[4] yüen-gu
a reason.

Interrogative Adverbs.

When 幾時 gi shï
when? at what time?

你幾時來的 ni gi-shï lai dy?
when did you come.

多偺 do dzan
when.

多偺說的 do dzan shwoh dy?
when was it said?
(*do dzan* is almost patois).

Where 那裏 na-li
where?

他在那裏 ta dzai na-li
where is he?

他從那裏來的 ta tsung na-li lai dy?
where did he come from?

你到那裏去 ni dao na-li chü?
where are you going?

Why 爲甚麼 wei-shen-mo
why?

你爲甚麼打他 ni wei-shen-mo da ta?
why did you strike him?

爲甚麼緣故 wei-shen-mo güen-gu?
for what reason?

How Often 幾回 gi hwei?
how often?

好幾回 hao gi-hwei
a good many times.

先生幾回來過上海 hsien-seng gi-hwei lai go Shanghai, *how often have you, Sir, been to Shanghai?*

你幾回辦了這樣的公事 ni gi hwei ban-liao dje yang dy gung-szï; *how often have you managed an affair of this kind?*

How Many 幾[3]個[4] gi-go
how many a few?

when the expected answer is a small number as the years of a child's age

你[3]有[3]幾[3]歲[4] ni yu gi sui
how old are you?

我[3]五[3]歲[3]了[3] o wu sui liao
I am five years old.

HOW MANY 多[4]少[1] do shao *how many?* when the answer expected is a large number.

有[3]多[1]少[3]錢[2] yu do shao ch'ien, *how much money is there?*

一[1]百[3]多[1]塊[4] ih beh do kwai, *more than a hundred dollars.*

Interrogative Sentences.

As has been stated the usual way to ask a question in Chinese is to make an affirmation and then qualify it by a negative as:—

他有錢沒有 ta yu chien muh-yu, *he has money, has he not?*

他是個好人不是 ta shï go hao ren buh shï, *he is a good man, is he not?*

你會寫字不會 ni hwei hsie dzï buh hwei, *are you able to write or not?*

Negative sentences presume an affirmative answer.

這不是做壞了麼 dje buh shï dzo hwai liao ma, *is this not spoiled in the making?*

這不是太貴麼 dje buh shï tai gwei mo, *is this not too dear?*

It is presumed that the answer to these sentences will be "Yes, it is spoiled; it is too dear."

The interrogative 豈 chi, placed at the commencement of a negative sentence makes a strong affirmative.

他豈沒有錢麼 ta chi muh-yu chien mo, *has he no money?* The tone and structure of the question assumes that he has plenty of money.

他豈不是好人麼 ta chi buh shï hao ren ma, *is he not a good man?* Suggesting that if *he* is not a good man there are no good men.

不[1]是[4] buh shï, *is not*, and 沒[2]有[3] muh yu, *have not*, are often used as interrogatives.

這[4]話[4]是[4]你[3]說[1]的[4]不[1]是[4] dje hwa shï ni shwoh dy buh shï, *did you say these words or did you not?*

不是我說的 buh shï o shwoh dy, *I did not say them.*

是不是你做 shī buh shī ni dzo, *did you or did you not do it?*

我沒有做 o muh yu dzo, *I did not do it.*

我們中國話先生懂不懂 o men djung gwoh hwa hsien-seng dung buh dung, *do you, Sir, understand our Chinese language or not?*

我懂一點 o dung ih dien, *I understand a little.*

中國字你能寫不能寫 djung gwoh dzī ni neng hsie buh neng hsie, *can you write Chinese characters or can you not?*

我寫不多少 o hsie buh do shao, *I cannot write many.*

他這個話是甚麼意思 ta dje go hwa shī shen mo i-szī, *what does he mean by these words?*

Interrogative Pronouns and Adverbs.

那一個 nao ih go *who.*	那一個的 na ih go dy *whose.*
誰 shui *who.*	誰的 shui dy *whose.*
甚麼 shen-mo *what.*	甚麼人的 shen-mo ren dy *whose.*
甚麼人 shen-mo ren *who.*	你作甚麼 ni dzoh shen-mo *what are you doing?*

門外是那一個 men wai shī na ih go, *who is outside the door?*

這個車子是那一個的 dje-go che-dz shī na ih go dy *whose cart is this?*

他是誰 ta shī shui, *who is he?*

那是誰的馬 na shī shui dy ma, *whose horse is that?*

甚麼事 shen-mo szī, *what is it?* (What is the matter?)

你是甚麼人 ni shī shen-mo ren, *who are you?* (rude)

他是甚麼人的朋友 ta shī shen-mo ren dy peng-yu, *whose friend is he?*

你爲甚麼這樣做 ni wei shen-mo dje yang dzo, *why do you act thus?*

他爲甚麼說這話 ta wei shen-mo shwoh dje hwa, *why did he say that?*

Studying these sentences the student will note that the order of the words in the Chinese sentence is the reverse of that used in English. The English sentence "Who is outside the door?" becomes in Chinese "Door outside who?" The interrogative word in Chinese being placed, like the interrogative sign in English, at the end of the sentence.

何 ho, is the interrogative pronoun *what*. It follows the verb and precedes the noun.

何人 ho ren, *what man (is this)?*

何故 ho gu, *what reason?*

是何言哉 shï ho yen dzai, *what words are these?*

如何 ru ho, is the interrogative adverb *how*. Like most adverbs it precedes the verb.

如何辦呢 ru ho ban ni, *how (shall we) manage?*

如何是好 ru ho shï hao, *how can it be helped?*

何[2]如[2] ho ru is a variant of the above. It is usually followed by 爲 wei, the verb *to be*.

何如儉省爲好 ho ru gien seng wei hao, *how much better to be economical?*

何如不說爲妙 ho ru buh shwoh wei miao, *how much better to be silent?*

怎[3]麼[1] dzen-mo has the same meaning and is used in the same way as 何 ho, *how*.

怎麼樣 dzen-mo yang, (*how fashion?*) *in what way?*

怎麼做法 dzen-mo dzo fah, *how do you do it?*

你爲甚麼這樣做 ni wei shen-mo dje yang dzo, *why do you act thus?*

他爲甚麼說這話 ta wei shen-mo shwoh dje hwa, *why did he say that?*

LESSON XII.

Relative Pronouns.

There are two relative pronouns in common use. They are 的[4] dih and 所[3] so, and are translated *who*, *which*, or *that*, as the exigencies of the sentence demand.

Colloquially 所 so is always followed by 的 dih which, in this construction, is the possessive particle. 所 so differs from the relative pronoun in English in that the noun on which it depends stands at the end of the sentence. Thus in the clause 他所說的話 ta so shwoh dy hwa, *the words which he spoke*. In English, the noun "words" precedes and is the antecedent of the relative pronoun "which." In Chinese the noun 話 hwa, *words*, is placed at the end of the sentence and so cannot be called the antecedent though it stands in the same relation to the pronoun as in English.

Order of the words in the relative clause.

The order of the words is invariable. The relative pronoun precedes the verb and the noun on which it depends is placed at the end of the clause.

他所說的話 ta so shwoh dy hwa, *the words which he spoke*.
我所做的事情 o so dzo dy szï-ching, *the things which I did*.
你所買的書 ni so mai dy shu, *the books which you bought*.

The function of the possessive particle in the clause.

The adjective particle preceding the noun shows that the first part of the clause is an adjective.

	Adjective.		*Noun.*
他所說的	ta so shwoh dy *the-which-he-spoke*	話	hwa *words.*
你所買的	ni so mai dy, *the-you-which-bought*	東西	dung-hsi *things.*
馬所吃的	ma so chïh dy, *the-horse-which-eaten*	草	tsao *grass.*

Relative clause in its relation to the sentence.

The relative clause may be either the subject, object, or complement according as it precedes or follows the predicate in the sentence.

SUBJECT.	PREDICATE.	COMPLEMENT.
這 dje *these*	就是 dziu shï *really are*	他所說的話 ta so shwoh dy hwa *the words which he spoke*
小先生 hsiao hsien-seng *the young master*	正是 djeng shï *actually is*	他自己所生的兒子 ta dzi-gi so seng dy er-dz *her own begotten son*
他所說的話 ta so shwoh dy hwa *the words which he spoke*	盡是 dzin shï *were entirely*	假的 gia dy *false*
聖書所載的道理 sheng shu so dzai dy dao-li *the doctrines contained in the Bible*	無不 wu buh *none not (all are)*	好 hao *good*

所 So also contains the idea of totality.

船所到的地方 chwan so dao dy di-fang
all the places at which the ship arrived.

世界所有的國度 shi-giai so yu dy kwoh-du
all the kingdoms of the world.

公司所有的本錢 gung-szï so yu dy ben-chien
all the capital of the company.

Note:—In classical or documentary writings 所 so is not necessarily followed by 的 dih or the corresponding sign of the genitive 之 djï. Nevertheless the grammatical construction is the same, the classical being merely an abbreviated style, e.g.,

Colloquial, 聖書所載的道理無不好 sheng-shu so dzai dy dao-li wu buh hao; *all the doctrines contained in the Bible are good.*

Classical, 聖書所載無不善 sheng-shu so dzai wu buh shan; *all that the Bible contains is good.*

Colloquial, 他所說的話都是實在的 ta so shwoh dy hwa du shï shïh-dzai dy; *all the words that he spoke were true.*

Classical, 口中所言皆實 kou djung so yeu giai shïh; *all that he said was true.*

的 Dih used alone as a relative pronoun.

他吃的是蔬菜 ta chïh-dy shï su tsai; *what he ate was vegetable relish.*

我唸的是外國書 o nien-dy shï wai-gwoh shu; *what I am reading is a foreign book.*

It is probable that the original construction of these sentences was

他吃的菜是蔬菜 ta chih dy tsai shï su tsai; *the relish he ate was vegetable relish.*

我唸的書是外國書 o nien dy shu shï wai-gwoh shu; *the book I read is a foreign book.*

To avoid repetition the first noun in the sentence is omitted and dih takes its place and is therefore, in this construction, a pronoun.

LESSON XIII.

THE VERB.

The verb is extremely simple. There is no inflexion; the moods and tenses are formed by the addition of auxiliary verbs and particles.

Present Tense,

做^4 dzo *to do.*

我^{3}做^4 o dzo *I do.*	我^{3}們^{2}做^4 o men dzo *we do.*
你^{3}做^4 ni dzo *thou doest.*	你^{3}們^{2}做^4 ni men dzo *you do.*
他^{1}做^4 ta dzo *he does.*	他^{1}們^{2}做^4 ta men dzo *they do.*

走³ dzou
to walk.

我³走³ o dzou
I walk.

你³走³ ni dzou
thou walkest.

他¹走³ ta dzou
he walks.

我³們²走³ o men dzou
we walk.

你³們²走³ ni-men dzou
you walk.

他²們²走³ ta-men dzou
they walk.

And so on. The verbs are all regular.

請³ ching
please; to invite.

懂² dung
to understand.

寫³ hsie
to write.

講³ giang
to speak.

把¹ ba
to take.

來² lai
to come.

去⁴ chü
to go.

開¹ kai
to open.

帶⁴ dai
to carry in the hand.

受⁴ shou
to receive.

給⁴ gih
to give.

拏² na
to grip, to carry.

挑¹ tiao
to carry on a pole.

抬² tai
to carry between two.

動⁴ dung
to move.

關¹ gwan
to shut a gate.

進⁴ dzin
to enter.

入³ ruh
to go in.

送⁴ sung
to present; to accompany.

起³ chi
to raise up.

到⁴ dao
to arrive at.

行² hsing
to walk.

行²走³ hsing-dzou
to walk.

Past Tense. The particle 了³ liao, *ended* or the particle 的⁴ dih—which we have met with so frequently in other connections—attached to the verb forms the past tense.

了 liao is, in its primary meaning, the verb *to finish* but when joined to a principal verb it is an auxiliary marking the completion of the verbal action. It is so commonly used in this sense that it has come to be regarded as a particle indicating the past tense.

我³做⁴了³ o dzo liao
I did.

你³做⁴了³ ni dzo liao
thou didst.

他¹做⁴了³ ta dso liao
he did.

我們做了 o men dzo liao
we did.

你們做了 ni men dzo liao
you did.

他們做了 ta men dzo liao
they did.

請他來 tsing ta lai, *ask him to come.*

我請了他來 o tsing-liao ta lai, *I asked him to come.*

開門請他進來 kai men tsing ta dzin lai, *open the door and ask him to come in.*

門開了他進來了 men kai-liao, ta dzin lai-liao, *the door is opened; he has come in.*

那一個進來 na ih go dzin lai, *who came in?*

沒有人進來了 muh-yu ren dzin lai-liao, *nobody came in.*

The past tense formed by adding the particle 的[4] dih to *the verb.*

Present	說 shwoh *say.*	做 dzo *do.*	買 mai *buy.*
Past	說的 shwoh dih *said.*	做的 dzo dih *did.*	買的 mai dih *bought.*

這是你做的嗎 dje shï ni dzo dih ma, *did you do this?*

不是我做的 buh shï o dzo dih, *it was not I who did it.*

這個字是你寫的麽 dje go dzï shï ni hsie dih mo, *did you write these characters?*

In England in Shakespeare's day to "thou" a man—to address him by the second personal pronoun—was to insult him. In China 你 ni *thou* is used sparingly or to inferiors only. The last sentence, written above, if addressed to an equal, would be more politely expressed thus:—

這個字是你先生寫的麽 dje-go dzï shï ni hsien-seng hsie dy mo, *were these characters written by you, Sir?*

The Past Tense formed by the use of auxiliaries.

The past tense of a verb is often indicated by the use of a word denoting completion which is attached to the verb much as an auxiliary verb is in English. But it is to be noted that while the auxiliary precedes the principal verb in English, in Chinese it follows it.

Amongst the most commonly used of such auxiliaries are 好[3] hao, *well;* 完[2] wan, *finished;* 畢[4] bih, *ended;* 成[2] cheng, *completed;* 全[2] tsüen, *perfect;* and 到[4] dao, *arrived.* When used thus those words might be construed as adverbs but as the adverb usually precedes the verb it is simpler and better to regard them as part of the verb itself, indeed, as we have called certain double nouns compound nouns these might be called compound verbs.

The verb in its simplest form is 洗 hsi, *to wash*.
The past tense is 洗了 hsi-liao, *washed*.
The compound from is 洗好了 hsi hao-liao, *washed completely*.

衣服洗好了沒有 i-fuh hsi hao-liao muh yu, *are the clothes washed (completely washed) or not?*

早已洗好了 dzao i hsi hao-liao, *all washed long ago.*

書讀完了沒有 shu duh wan-liao muh yu, *have you finished your book yet?* Literally. Is your book read to the end yet?

已經讀完了 i-ging duh wan-liao, *it is already finished.*

公事辦畢了嗎 gung-szï ban bih liao ma, *is your business finished yet?*

他能做成了嗎 ta neng dzo cheng-liao ma, *can he complete the work?*

他的滿面紅漲起來了 ta dy man mien hung dzang chi lai liao, *her whole face flushed red.* 漲起來了 is the verb.

LESSON XIV.

The Imperfect.

The imperfect, or continuous, tense is not well marked in Chinese. In fact each of the tenses depends on auxiliary verbs, adverbs and particles to make its meaning clear and unambiguous. The character 着[2] djoh, *to place*, when used as a particle, may be taken as the sign of the imperfect though it is also used as a sign of the past. When 着 djoh is used alone it is a principal verb; it then precedes its object and has, in a measure, the sense of the imperative mood.

着[2] djoh, as a principal verb.

着力 djoh lih *put forth strength.*	着上些鹽 djoh shang hsie yen *add a little salt to it.*
着意 djoh i *give attention.*	着一點醋 djoh ih dien tsu *add a little vinegar*

火着了 ho djoh-liao, *the fire is alight.*

房子着了火 fang-dze djoh-liao ho, *the house has caught fire.*

When 着 djoh, follows another verb it is a particle and denotes that the action is continuous.

水流着甚快 shui liu-djoh shen kwai, *the water flows very quickly*, i.e., the water flows and continues flowing.

拏着 na-djoh, *hold* (and continue holding) *it.*

他睡着了 ta shwui-djoh joh liao, *he is asleep.*

女人背着臉 nü ren bei-djoh lien, *the woman turned away her face.*

孩子仰着頭 hai-dz yang-djoh tou, *the child lifted up his head.*

這個柴火燒不着 dje-go chai-ho shao buh djoh, *this fire-wood won't burn.*

The Imperative.

The particle 罷[4] ba *stop* is the sign of the imperative. It is placed immediately after the verb as 來[2]罷[4] lai ba, *come* 去[4]罷[4] chü ba, *go*, but 罷 ba is an imperative of such peremptory force that it can only be used in addressing those from whom one has a right to expect obedience.

快[4]去[4]罷[4] kwai chü ba *go quickly; begone.*	給[4]我[3]罷[4] gih o ba *give it to me.*
拏[2]來[1]罷[4] na lai ba *bring it here.*	罷[4]了[3]罷[4]了[3] ba liao ba *enough; finished; that will do.*

Structure of sentence in imperative mood.

The sentence in the imperative mood has a distinctive structure of its own. The first word in such sentences is always either the verb, which may be preceded by its adverb, or the second personal pronoun, the subject of the sentence.

快去喊他來 kwai chü han ta lai, *go quickly and call him.*

你不要去 ni buh yao chü, *you need not go.*

你帶他去罷 ni dai ta chü ba, *you take him* (Note 帶 dai which means "to carry" is also used meaning to lead)

叫事務擺桌子 giao szï-fu bai djoh-dz, *tell the servant to lay the table.*

請先生到書房來 ching hsien-seng tao shu fang lai, *ask the teacher to come into the library.*

快[4] kwai
quick.

背[1] bei
the back; to turn the back.

流[2] liu
to flow.

睡[4] shui
to sleep.

睡[4]覺[4] shui-giao
to sleep.

仰[3] yang
to lift up the head.

柴[2]火[3] chai-ho
fire-wood.

臉[3] lien
the face.

早[3]已[3] dzao i
long ago, early.

已[3]經[1] i-ging
already.

工[1]夫[1] gung-fu
time, leisure.

公[1]事[4] gung-szï
public business.

辦[4] ban
to manage.

洗[3] hsi
to wash.

叫 giao
to call, to cause.

得[2] deh
to obtain.

認[3]得[2] ren-deh
to recognise.

曉[3]得[2] hsiao-deh
to know.

記[4]得[2] gi-deh
to remember.

做[4]得[2] dzo-deh
do; may be done.

捨[3]得[2] she-deh
give; may be given.

捨[3]不[1]得[2] she-buh-deh
loth to give.

罪[4] dzui
sin.

得[2]罪[4] deh-dzui
to offend; sin against.

忘[1]記[4] wang-gi
to forget.

雙[1] shwang
double.

一[1]雙[1] ih shwang
a pair.

遠[3] yüen
distant.

近[4] gin
near.

告[4]訴[4] gao-su
to tell.

The verb 得[2] deh, *to obtain*, is commonly used as an auxiliary and then forms a distinctive and very useful idiom. When 得 deh, is placed after the principal verb it indicates that the action may, or, ought to be done. When it is placed with a negative before the verb it indicates that the action cannot or must not be done. It might be called the sign of the potential mood.

我不得去 o buh deh chü, *I cannot go.*

我去不得 o chü buh deh, *I may not go.*

這個話說不得 dje-go hwa shwoh buh deh, *these words may not be said.*

你想這個事做得做不得 ni hsiang dje-go szï dzo-deh dzo buh deh, *do you think this may be done or may not be done?*

他沒有工夫不得做 ta muh-yu gung-fu, buh deh dzo, *he has no time: he cannot do it.*

這個人你認得不認得 dje-go ren ni ren deh buh ren-deh, *do you know this man?*

洋錢的眞假你認得不認得 yang chien dy djen gia ni ren-deh buh ren-deh? *can you recognise good and bad dollars?*

他捨不得錢 ta she-buh-deh chien, *he begrudges money.*

得罪你先生 deh-dzui ni hsien-seng, *I beg your pardon, Sir.*

叫他把我的東西帶來 giao ta ba o-dy dung-hsi dai lai, *tell him to bring my things.*

這個話是那一個告訴你 dje-go hwa shï na-ih go gao su ni, *who told you this?*

他告訴我我沒有聽見 ta gao-su o, o muh-yu ting-gien, *he told me but I did not hear.*

他睡覺了我睡不着 ta shui-giao liao, o shui buh djoh, *he is asleep, but I cannot sleep.*

你爲甚麼不能睡 ni wei shen-mo buh neng shwui, *why can't you sleep?*

因爲思想太多 yin-wei szï-hsiang tai do, *because of a multitude of thoughts.*

他辦了甚麼公事 ta ban-liao shen-mo gung-szï, *what public business does he manage?*

我走不動 o dzou buh dung, *I cnnnot walk (farther).*

拉不動他了 la buh dung ta liao, *I cannot pull him.*

LESSON XV

The Perfect Tense.

The Perfect is formed by using the verb, 過 go, *to pass over*, as a particle following the verb in the same way as 着 djoh, is used to form the imperfect. (See page 64.)

As a principal verb 過 go is used in such sentences as 過去 go chü, *go over*. 他過去了 ta go chü liao, *he has gone over*. 我過不過去 o go buh go chü, *I cannot get over*. 過日子 go rĭh dzĭ, *to pass the days; to live*.

As an auxiliary 過 go, is attached to the principal verb and indicates that the action has been finished.

這個話說過了 dje-go hwa shwoh go liao
this has been said.

東西買過了 dung-hsi mai go liao
the things have been bought.

事情辦過了 szĭ-ching ban go liao
the matters have been arranged.

他那位老先生已經來過了 ta na wei lao hsien-seng i-ging lai go liao
that old gentleman has been here before.

上海我來過一回 Shanghai o lai go ih hwei
I have been once before to Shanghai.

Future Tense.

The future is formed by using the verb 要[4] yao, *want* or *will*, as an auxiliary. Note that it precedes the principal verb.

我要到你那裏去 o yao dao ni na-li chü
I want to (or, I will) go to your place.

他要買幾個東西 ta yao mai gi-go dung-hsi
he wants to buy some things

我要打他 o yao da ta
I will beat him.

Sometimes 要 yao, is omitted and implied as 我明天去 o ming tien chü, *I shall go to-morrow*

他明天來 ta ming tien lai
he will come to-morrow

向^4 hsiang
towards.

向^{4}來^2 hsiang lai
hitherto.

後^{4}來^2 hou lai
afterwards.

過^{1}犯^4 go fan
transgression.

早^{3}上^4 dzao shang
morning.

晚^{3}上^4 wan shang
evening.

今^{1}天^1 gin tien
to-day.

昨^{2}天^1 dzoh tien
yesterday.

當^{1}心^1 dang hsin
be careful.

留^{2}心^1 liu hsin
be careful.

賬^4 djang
an account.

擔^1 dan
a load.

行^{2}李^3 hsing-li
luggage.

人^{2}家^1 ren gia
other folks.

天^{1}下^4 tien hsia
everywhere; the Empire.

今^{1}年^2 gin nien
this year.

去^{4}年^2 chü nien
last year.

明^{2}年^2 ming nien
next year.

正^{1}月^4 djeng yüeh
the first moon.

二^{4}月^4 er yüeh
the second moon.

臘^{4}月^4 lah yüeh
the twelfth moon.

本^{3}事^4 ben szï
ability.

舖^{4}子 pu dz
a shop.

店^4 dien
a shop.

太^{4}陽^2 tai yang
the sun.

月^{4}亮^4 yüeh-liang
the moon.

星^1 hsing
a star.

處^3 chu
a place.

好^{3}處^3 hao chu
an advantage.

上 shang, *above* and 下 hsia, *below* are used in relation to time, in the sense of "last" and "next."

上禮拜一日 shang li-bai ih rïh
last Monday.

下禮拜三日 hsia li-bai san rïh
next Wednesday.

他去年到我家來過 ta chü nien dao o gia lai go
he came to my house last year.

你要小心不要大意 ni yao hsiao-hsin buh yao da-i
be careful; don't be careless.

人家的賬要當心 ren-gia dy djang yao dang hsin
be careful about people's accounts.

到六月要熱起來 dao luh yüeh yao reh chi lai
when the sixth moon comes it will be hot.

今天沒有太陽不曉得晚上有月亮沒有 gin tien muh-yu tai yang buh hsiao-deh wan-shang yu yüeh-liang muh yu
there is no sun to-day; it is not certain whether there will be a moon this evening or not.

你向來沒有做過這事 ni hsiang-lai muh yu dzo go dje szĭ
you have not done this before.

你要早上去還是晚上去呢 ni yao dzao-shang chü hai shï wan-shang chü ni
will you go in the morning or will you go in the evening?

我後來去 o hou lai chü
I shall go afterwards.

LESSON XVI.

The Subjunctive Mood.

The subjunctive mood has only one tense or, rather, it has the same form for the present and future tenses. It is formed by the characters 可[3] 以[3] ko-i, *may*, preceding the verb.

The subjunctive is an important mood. Foreigners often speak to the Chinese in an imperative tone which they little intend to use, and which is much resented simply because they are not aware of the harsh nature of the language used. A free use of the subjunctive avoids this.

你可以請他來 ni ko-i ching ta lai
you might ask him to come.

你要去就可以去 ni yao chü dziu ko-i chü
if you want to go you may go.

告訴他明天可以來 gao su ta ming-tien ko-i lai
say that he might come to-morrow.

我那個行李可以拏來 o na-go hsing-li ko-i na lai
you might bring my luggage here.

There are a few words which act as auxiliaries in the formation of this mood. These are 許[3] hsü, to *promise, may*; 或[4] hwoh, *either; perhaps*; 或[4] 者[3] hwoh-dje, *whether; perhaps*, 恐[3] 怕[4] kung-pa; *fear; lest; perhaps.*

許他今天來也許明天來 hsü ta gin-tien lai ye hsü ming-tien lai, *he may come to-day or he may come to-morrow.*

許他有也許他沒有 hsü ta yu ye hsü ta muh yu *he may have it or he may not.*

或大或小皆可 hwoh da hwoh hsiao giai ko *either large or small will do.*

或者他能做我不能說一定 hwoh-dje ta neng dzo o buh neng shwoh ih ding, *perhaps he can do it; I cannot certainly say.*

恐怕做不成 kung-pa dzo buh cheng *I fear he cannot finish it.*

The Optative Mood.

There is no word which may be taken as the sign of the optative but there are many words that express a wish. The commonest are

巴不得 ba buh deh *would that.*

情願 ching yüen *heartily wish so.*

但願 dan yüen *only wish* (that it might be so).

巴不得他回來 ba buh deh ta hwei lai *would that he would return.*

但願如此 dan yüen ru-tzï *would that it might be so.*

我情願幫助你 o ching-yüen bang-dzu ni *I very much wish to assist you.*

LESSON XVII.

The Passive voice.

被[4] bei, *a coverlet*, is used in its sense of *to suffer* or *to allow* as the sign of the passive voice. The order of the sentence is invariable. The subject is placed first, the verb last, and the sign of the passive in the middle. In other words the sentence is formed as in English.

房子被他賣了 fang-dz bei ta mai-liao *the house was sold by him.*

我被辱罵不輕 o bei ruh-ma buh ching *I was badly abused.*

這個話被我說過了 dje-go hwa bei o shwoh go liao *this has been said by me.*

There are a few auxiliaries which also form the passive: they are 挨[1] ai, *to suffer;* 受[4] shou, *to receive;* 叫[4] giao, *to cause;* and 給[4] gih, *to give.*

我們挨打被罵 o-men ai da bei ma
we suffered beating and were reviled.

諸位受過了他的責備 dju wei shou go liao ta dy dzeh-bei
each of you has suffered his rebukes.

孩子叫父母教訓好了 hai-dz giao fu mu giao hsün hao liao
the child was well taught by his parents.

老王給老虎吃了 lao wang gih lao hu chih liao
old Wang was eaten by the tiger.

喊[3] han
to call.

挑[1]夫[1] tiao fu
a coolie.

便[4] bien
handy.

方[1]便[4] fang bien
convenient.

和[2] ho
harmony; with.

同[2] tung
together.

比[3]方[1] bi-fang
for instance.

深[1] shen
deep.

淺[3] chien
shallow.

所[3]以[3] *so-i*
therefore.

定[4] ding
fixed.

定[4]規[1] ding-gwei
certainly.

豈 chi
an interrogative, can?

敢 gan
to dare.

豈[3]敢[3] chi-gan
I dare not; a polite refusal of a favour.

賤[4] dzien
unworthy.

古[3] gu
ancient.

今[1] *gin*
present.

姓[4] hsing
a name.

又[4] yu
also.

右[4] yu
right.

左[3] dzo
left.

賣[4] mai
to sell.

賣[3]買[4] mai-mai
business.

清[1]楚[3] ching-tsu
clear.

請[3]問[2] ching-wen
may I ask? (The proper way to ask a question.)

用[4] yung
use (verb).

用[4]處[4] yung-chu
use.

法[4] fah (fah-dz)
a plan.

等[3] deng
to wait.

待[4] dai
to treat; to wait.

肯[3] ken
willing.

愛[4] ai
love.

狠[3] hen
hate.

喜[3]歡[1] hsi-hwan
pleased.

高[1] gao
high.

低[1] di
low.

乾[1]淨[4] gan-dzing
clean.

骯[1]髒[1] ang-dzang
dirty.

反[3] fan
to reverse.

覆[4] fu
again.

也[3] ye
also.

你可以喊叫他來 ni ko-i han-giao ta lai.
you might call him (to come).

那個挑夫挑不動重東西 na-go tiao-fu tiao buh dung djung-dung-hsi
that coolie can't carry a heavy load.

我和你同去 o ho ni tung chü
I shall go with you.

比方他是好人 bi-fang ta shï hao ren
suppose he is a good man.

先生貴姓 hsien-seng gwei hsing
what, Sir, is your honourable name?

賤姓王 dzien sing Wang
my unworthy name is Wang.

請問這做甚麽用 ching wen dje dzo shen mo yung
may I ask what is the use of this?

等一等 deng ih deng
wait a bit.

他們待我甚好 ta-men dai o shen hao
they treated me very well.

所以我也應當待他們好 so-i o ye ying-dang dai ta-men hao
therefore I also ought to treat them well.

他做甚麽買賣 ta dzo shen-mo mai-mai
what business does he do?

沒有法子 muh-yu fah-dz
there is no help for it.

LESSON XVIII.

ADVERBS. The verb being without inflection and, as we have seen, defective in many of its forms, the language is more dependent on adverbs for expressing the tenses than are those languages in which the verb is inflected.

The Present. Verbs in the present tense do not need to be modified by any adverb to express the sense of time; 剛 Gang, *now*, and 纔 tsai, *just now*, both indicate the present; yet, when we say 我纔明白 o tsai ming-beh, *I now understand;* or 我剛到的 o kang dao dy, *I have just come;* the "understanding" and the "come" are both thought of as completed actions and so the adverbs really indicate the past tense.

Past Tense

他剛纔去了 ta gang-tsai chü liao
he has this moment gone.

他此刻纔來 ta tsĭ keh tsai lai
he has this moment just come.

我剛纔到了 o gang-tsai dao liao
I have just come.

The Imperfect Tense 正 djeng, *upright, exact,* is often used to modify a verb and indicate that the action is still incomplete.

正吃著飯 djeng chĭh-djoh fan
just while eating food.

他們正說話的時候 ta-men djeng shwoh hwa dy shĭ-hou
just while they were speaking.

說話之間 shwoh hwa djĭ gien
while speaking (a somewhat classical phrase).

Future Tense.

要[4] yao
will.

就[4] dziu
thereupon.

將[1] dziang
presently.

再[4] dzai
again.

馬[3]上[4] ma-shang
quickly.

一[1]刻[1] ih-keh
in a moment.

These are all adverbs modifying the verb in the future tense.

我就要去 o dziu yao chü
I am just about to go.

他將要走 ta dziang yao dzou
he is just going to start.

我們馬上要去 o-men ma-shang yao chü
we will go in a moment (馬上 ma-shang, as quickly as a horse gallops past).

過一天再來 go ih tien dzai lai
come again another day.

他一刻就來 ta ih-keh dziu lai
he will be here in a minute.

Perfect Tense.

已經 i-ging *already* and 早已 dzao-i *long ago*
are adverbs, modifying the verb in the perfect tense.

他已經來過了 ta i-ging lai go liao
he has been here already.

早已做過了 dzao-i dzo go liao
has been done long ago.

我的書早已讀畢了 o dy shu dzao-i duh bih liao
my book has been read to a finish long ago.

現[4]在[4] hsien dzai
just now.

古[3]時[2]候[4] gu shï-hou
anciently.

常[2] chang
constantly.

常[2]常[2]的 chang-chang dy
constantly.

時[2]時[2] shï-shï
constantly.

時[2]時[2]刻[1]刻[1] shï-shï keh-keh
every moment.

此[3]刻[1] tzï keh
immediately.

方[1]刻[1] fang keh
immediately.

立[4]刻[1] lih keh
immediately.

正[1]好[3] djeng-hao
just right.

將[1]好[3] dziang-hao
exactly right.

第[4]一[1] di-ih
first.

第[4]二[4] di-er
second.

第[4]三[1] di-san
third, etc.

少[3]有[3] shao yu
seldom.

少[3]見[4] shao gien
seldom seen.

但[4] dan
only.

只[3] djï
only.

實[2]在[4] shïh dzai
truly.

陡[3]然[2] dou ran
suddenly.

雖^{1}然^{2} sui-ran
although.

自^{4}然^{2} dzï-ran
certainly.

當^{1}然^{2} dang-ran
fitting, right.

天^{1}然^{2} tien ran
naturally.

幾^{3}時^{2} gi-shï
when.

甚^{4}麽^{1}時^{2}候^{4} shen-mo shï-hou
when.

一^{1}霎^{4}子^{3} ih shah dz
in a minute.

一^{1}霎^{4}時^{2} ih shah shï
instantly.

不^{4}長^{2}不^{4}短^{3} buh chang buh dwan
not long and not short; just right.

快^{4}樂^{4} kwai-loh
happily.

憂^{1}悶^{4} yu-men
sorrowful.

憂^{1}愁^{2} yu-tsou
sorrow.

曾^{2} tseng
already.

未^{4}曾^{2} wei-tseng
never.

起^{3} chi
to raise up.

擔^{1}當^{1}不^{4}起^{3} dan dang buh chi
can't bear it.

好^{3}比^{3} hao bi
supposing.

Comparison of adverbs.

The degrees of comparison of adverbs are formed in the same way as those of adjectives. (See pp. 40 and 44.)

快^{4} kwai
quick.

快^{4}些^{3} kwai-hsie
quicker.

最^{4}快^{4} dzui kwai
quickest.

甚^{4}快^{4} shen kwai
very quick.

快^{4}一^{1}點^{3} kwai ih-dien
a little quicker.

太^{4}快^{4} tai-kwai
too quick.

NOTE:—Students of Chinese agree that in translations from Chinese into another language the *idea* in the sentence is to be clearly expressed but the grammatical structure of the sentence cannot be rigidly adhered to. Thus in the first example given in Lesson xviii of the adverb modifying the past tense we have the sentence 他剛纔去了 ta gang tsai chü liao, *he this moment went* or *he has this moment gone.* One of those sentences is in the past, the other in the perfect tense in English, but either is a correct translation of the Chinese. The same idea is expressed by either form of speech and as the tenses are not recognised in Chinese, either is correct. These lessons are cast in the grammatical form with which the English student is familiar in order that he may readily see how the different parts of speech modify the meaning of the sentence, but it is not to be inferred that the translation of a sentence is wrong if the English does not reproduce in exact grammatical form the Chinese equivalent. Neither must the student, as has already been pointed out, study the grammar of Chinese in the English translations of the Chinese sentences. The verb, and the adverbs which modify it, are to be studied in the Chinese characters.

If the foregoing sentences are thus studied the student will note that adverbs precede the verbs which they modify and auxiliary verbs and verbal particles follow the principal verbs.

我的書早巳讀畢了 o dy shu dzao-i duh bih liao, *my book has been read to a finish long ago*

the subject is 我的書 *my book*

the verb is 讀 *read*

the auxiliary is 畢 *finished*

the final verbal particle is 了 denoting completion

the adverb is 早己 *long ago*

The construction can be shown in a diagram

Subject	Adverb	Predicate
我的書	早己	讀畢了

Chinese grammar is very simple and regular but it cannot be learned from English translations of Chinese sentences.

LESSON XIX.

Adverbial and Adjectival Phrases.

When the particle 的 dy, is placed between an adverb and a verb it makes the whole phrase modify the verb. When it comes between a descriptive phrase and a noun it makes the phrase qualify the noun. It is thus either an adverbial or adjectival particle according as it is used to qualify a noun or modify a verb.

Adverbial.

好好的作 hao hao dy dzoh *do it properly.*

快快的跑 kwai kwai dy pao *run quickly.*

慢慢的走 man man dy dzou *go slowly.*

明明的說 ming ming dy shwoh *speak clearly.*

Note the duplication of the adverbs 好好 hao hao, 慢慢 man man, 快快 kwai kwai, 明明 ming ming. This is a very common construction and examples might be multiplied indefinitely.

他暗暗的想 ta an an dy hsiang *he secretly thought.*

他一個人往外悄悄的走了 ta ih go ren wang wai tsiao-tsiao dy dzou liao, *he went out by himself and secretly went away.*

你必恭恭敬敬的接待他們 ni bih gung gung ging ging dy dzieh-dai ta-men, *you must receive them very politely.*

彼得不住的叩門 bi-deh buh dju dy kou men, *Peter continued knocking.*

If we make a diagram of these sentences we shall see at a glance the relation of the component parts to each other.

Subject.	Adverb.	Predicate.	Object.
他	暗暗的	想	
他	一個人 悄悄的 往外	走了	
你	必恭恭敬敬的	接待	他們
彼得	不住的	叩	門

Adjectival.

他是個假冒爲善的人 ta shï go gia mao wei shan dy ren, *he is a hypocritical man.*

你不要說半明半暗的話 ni buh yao shwoh ban ming ban an dy hwa, *do not talk ambiguous language.*

這是一個良善忠心的用人 dje-shī ih-go liang shan djung hsin dy yung ren, *this is a good and faithful servant.*

我要一個寬綽乾淨的房間 o yao ih go kwan-choh gan-dzing dy fang-gien, *I want a large clean room.*

Subject.	Predicate.	Adjective.	Object.
他	是	個假冒爲善的	人
你	不要說	半明半暗的	話
這	是	一個良善忠心的	用人
我	要	一個寬綽乾淨的	房間

Various uses of 的 dy. We have seen this character used in so many different ways that a recapitulation is necessary.

When 的 dy follows a personal pronoun as 我的 o-dy, *mine;* 你的 ni-dy, *yours;* 他的 ta-dy, *his;* 的 dy is the possessive particle.

When it follows a verb in sentences such as 我說的 o shwoh-dy, *I said it;* 他做的 ta dzo-dy, *he did it;* 你買的 ni mai-dy, *you bought it;* 的 dy is a sign of the past tense.

When it follows a name or proper noun in sentences such as 有一個姓王的來了 yu ih-go hsing Wang dy lai liao, *a man who is named Wang has come,* 的 dy is a relative pronoun for it means "*who*" and has an antecedent "*Wang*."

When it joins a phrase to a verb as in the sentence 我實實在在的告訴你 o shih-shih dzai-dzai dy gao-su ni, *I tell you truly,* 的 dy is an adverbial particle for it attaches the modifying phrase to the verb.

When it joins a phrase to a noun as in the sentence 文武斌斌的君子 wen wu bin bin dy gün-dz, *A gentleman skilled in the arts of peace and war,* 的 dy is an adjectival particle for it attaches the qualifying phrase to the noun.

相[1]干[1] hsiang-gan *business; concern.*

隨[2]便[4] sui-bien *at your convenience.*

可[3]惜[3] ko-hsih *alas!*

彼[3]此[3] bi-tsī *mutually.*

力[4]氣[4] lih-chi *strength.*

撒[1]謊[4] sah-hwang *to lie* (make a false statement).

商[1]議[4] shang-i *discuss.*

繙[1] fan *translate.*

快[4]活[2] kwai-hoh *happily.*

貧[2]窮[2] pin-chiung *poor.*

吩[1]咐[4] fen-fu *command.*

憑[2]據[4] ping-gü *proof.*

爲[2]止[3] wei-djï *as a limit.*

應[1]許[3] ying-hsü *promise.*

糊[2]塗[2] hu-tu *stupid.*

指[3]望[4] djï-wang *hope.*

規[1]矩[3] gwei-gü *custom.*

大[4]概[4] da-gai *generally.*

享[3]福[2] hsiang-fuh *enjoy happiness.*

受[4]苦[3] shou-ku *suffer bitterness.*

學[2]問[2] hsioh-wen *learning.*

盼[4]望[4] pan-wang *expect.*

幫[1]助[4] bang-dzu *to assist.*

希[1]望[4] hsi-wang *expect.*

我們可以彼此幫助 o-men ko-i bi-tsï bang-dzu *we can mutually assist each other.*

富貴人應當幫助貧窮人 fu-gwei ren ying-dang bang-dzu pin-chiung ren, *the rich should help the poor.*

此地沒有這個規矩 tsï di muh-yu dje-go gwei-gü *there is no such custom here.*

有甚麼憑據 yu shen-mo ping-gü, *what proof is there?*

請你隨便來 ching ni sui-bien lai, *please come whenever it is convenient for you.*

糊塗人力氣大 hu-tu ren lih-chi da, *stupid people have great strength.*

請你把這個中國字繙出英文 ching ni ba dje-go djung-gwoh dzï fan chuh ying wen *please translate this Chinese document into English.*

LESSON XX.

Prepositions.

The commonest preposition in the language is 在 dzai. In its original sense this word is a verb and means *to be, to exist.* It is commonly used in this sense in the phrases :—

父母在不在 fu-mu dzai buh dzai *are your parents alive?*

父母不在了 fu-mu buh dzai liao *they are not*, i.e., *they are dead.*

父母都在 fu-mu du dzai (*my*) *parents are both alive.*

在 dzai used as a preposition.

在家 dzai gia *at home.*	在中國 dzai djung-gwoh *in China.*
在外 dzai wai (at) *outside.*	在外國 dzai wai-gwoh *abroad.*
在這裏 dzai dje-li *here.*	在那裏 dzai na-li *there.*

先生在家不在家 hsien-seng dzai gia buh dzai gia, *is the teacher at home?*

先生不在家 hsien-seng buh dzai gia, *he is not at home.*

在 dzai used with auxiliary prepositions.

When 在 dzai is used with other, or, auxiliary prepositions it is then a good example of that compound structure of the language which we have noted in nouns, adjectives, and verbs. When used thus 在 dzai, the principal preposition, precedes the noun and the auxiliary is placed after the noun. Thus in the sentence 書在桌子上 shu dzai djoh-dz shang, *the book is on the table*, the preposition is 在 dzai..............上 shang and the noun 桌子 djoh-dz is placed between the two parts of the compound preposition.

Note:—Grammatically it would be equally correct to construe 在 dzai in its primary sense as the verb *to be* but then we should be in a difficulty if we met with the answer 不是在桌子上 buh shī dzai djoh-dz shang, (*it*) *is not on the table* in which case we should have the two verbs 是 shī *to be* and 在 dzai *to be* clashing with each other in the sentence.

The commonest prepositions used with 在 dzai are

裏³ li *inside.*	後⁴ hou *behind.*
內⁴ nui *within.*	外⁴ wai *outside.*
上⁴ shang *above.*	左³ dzo *left.*
下⁴ hsia *below.*	右⁴ yu *right.*
前² chien *before.*	中¹ djung *middle.*

These are sometimes called post-positions because they are placed after the noun while 在 dzai is placed before it.

東西在桌子底下 dung-hsi dzai djoh-dz di hsia
the things are under the table.
The preposition is 在……下

先生在家裏 hsien-seng dzai gia li
the teacher is at home 在……裏

那地方在中國之外 na di-fang dzai djung-gwoh djï-wai
That place is outside of China 在…外

全家都住在一個大門之內 chüen gia du dju dzai ih-go da men djï nui, *the whole family dwells inside one big door*, i.e., one house-hold 在…內

Note that the verb *to be* is omitted in these sentences. The first sentence is not 東西是在桌子底下. The verb 是 shï is omitted though represented in the English translation by the word "are." This proves that though 在 dzai is used as a preposition it still retains its primitive verbal force.

There are some characters which are used to form a kind of double post-position. They are

頭[2] tou *a head.*	間[1] gien *between.*
面[4] mien *a face.*	邊[1] bien *the side.*

在水面上 dzai shui mien shang
on the surface of the water 在……面上

在房子裏頭 dzai fang-dz li-tou
inside the house 在……裏頭

在兩山中間 dzai liang shan djung-gien
between two hills 在……中間

在寶坐右邊 dzai bao dzo yu bien
on the right of the throne 在…右邊

Doubling the post-position adds nothing to the meaning of the sentence and the construction is avoided in classical writing but is very common in colloquial speech.

由[2] yu *from.*	入[4] ruh *into.*	自[3] dzï *from.*	從[2] tsung *from.*
到 dao *to.*	對[4] dui *to.*	向[4] hsiang *towards.*	往[3] wang *towards.*

以[2]前[2] i-chien *before.*

以[3]後[4] i-hou *afterwards.*

那[4]邊[1] na-bien *that side.*

這[4]邊[1] dje-bien *this side.*

酒[3]錢[2] dziu-chien *wine money; cumsha.*

茶[2]錢[2] cha chien *wine money; cumsha.*

一[1]齊[2] i-chi *the whole.*

在[4]內[4] dzai-nui *inside.*

在[4]外[4] dzai-wai *outside.*

算[4]賬[4] swan-djang *reckon an account.*

喝[1]茶[2] hoh-cha *drink tea.*

付[4]清[1] fu ching *paid in full.*

茶錢在外 cha-chien dzai wai, *gratuities extra.*

酒錢在內 dziu-chien dzai nui, *gratuities included.*

酒錢一齊都算在內 dziu-chien i-chi du swan dzai nui *all gratuities are included in the bill.*

Place of the preposition in the sentence.

我們到那裏去 o-men dao na-li chü, *where are we going?*

他從那裏來的 ta tsung na-li lai-dih, *where has he come from?*

你對他說 ni dui ta shwoh, *you say to him.*

到 dao 從 tsung and 對 dui are prepositions and while the order of the sentence is not the same as in English the preposition immediately precedes the noun, or substitute noun, which is its object.

除[2]非[1] chu-fei, *except.* 除非他自己來我不答應 chu-fei ta dzï-gi lai o buh dah-ying *unless he comes himself I will not consent.*

除 chu............以外 i-wai is an idiomatic phrase meaning *with the exception of.* The object is placed between the two parts of the compound preposition.

除你先生以外別人不能做 chu ni hsien-seng i-wai bieh ren buh neng dzo, *excepting you, sir, no other person can do it.*

除他以外沒有人知到 chu ta i-wai muh-yu ren djï-dao *excepting him no one knows.*

LESSON XXI.

Conjunctions.

Conjunctions are more sparingly used in Chinese than in English. The conjunction is frequently understood though unexpressed. The following list contains most of the more common colloquially used conjunctions but it might be considerably extended.

又[4] yu *and.*	也[3] ye *also.*	和[2] ho *with.*	同[2] tung *together.*	乃[3] nai *thereupon.*
但[4] dan *but.*	只[3] djï *only.*	奈[4] nai *but.*	以[3] i *in order to.*	與[3] yü *with.*
並[4] bing *also.*	連[2] lien *both.*	且[3] tsie *moreover*	若[4] roh *if*	然[2] ran *neverthe-* [*less.*

但[4]是[4] dan-shï *but, only.*	只[3]是[4] dji-shï *only, but.*	若[4]是[4] roh-shï *if.*
要[4]是[4] yao-shï *if.*	或[1]者[3] hwoh-dje *whether.*	雖[1]然[2] sui-ran *although.*
因[1]為[4] yin-wei *because.*	無[2]論[4] wu-lwen *whether.*	並[4]且[4] bing-tsie *moreover.*
況[4]且[3] kwang-tsie *still, more.*	又[4]且[3] yu-tsie *further.*	無[2]奈[4] wu-nai *but.*

我[3]也[3]去[4] o ye chu *I also shall go.*	他[1]又[4]來[2] ta yu lai *he also has come.*
我[3]同[2]你[3]去[4] o tung ni chu *I will go with you.*	若[4]是[4]他[1]來[2] roh-shï ta lai *if he comes.*

*又打他又罰他 yu da ta yu fah ta, *beat him and also punished him.*

他又急又氣又笑 ta yu gih yu chi yu hsiao, *he was excited and angry and also amused.*

他可以同你去 ta ko-i tung ni chü, *he may go with you.*

但是你要記得 dan-shï ni yao gi-deh, *but, you must remember.*

並且你要告訴他 bing tsie ni yao gao su ta, *moreover you must tell him.*

---

*The repetition of the conjunction adds emphasis to the sentence. Note the construction as given below.

我願意幫助你無奈我的力量不足 o yüen-i pang-dzu ni wu nai o dy lih liang buh dzuh, *I am willing to help you but my strength is insufficient.*

連他也要我服事嗎 lien ta ie yao o fuh-szĭ ma, *you want me also to serve him too?* (too is the equivalent of the Chinese conjunction 連 lien).

連本帶利都失了 lien ben dai li du shĭh liao, *both the capital and the profit were all lost.*

孩子連蹦帶跳跑去 hai-dz lien beng dai tiao pao chü, *the child both leaping and bounding ran off.*

連 lien *to connect* and 帶 dai *to bring* are examples of the compound principle which as we have seen inheres in every part of Chinese speech. The word is repeated or, as in this instance, the thought is repeated. Technically 連 lien and 帶 are correlative conjunctions.

A similar construction is

米甲的丈夫跟隨他 } mi-giah dy djang-fu ken sui ta
一面走路一面哭 } ih mien dzou lu ih mien kuh
Michal's husband followed her; weeping as he went (*2 Sam iii : 16*).

here the words 一面走，一面哭 ih mien dzou, ih mien kuh, may be translated *both walking and weeping*. More correctly the first 一面 is an adverb modifying the verb 走 the second 一面 modifies the verb 哭

事務隨走隨說 szĭ-fu sui dzou sui shwoh, *the servant then went saying*, (both walking and talking).

Negatives with verbal force

In Chinese sentences the verb *to be* is often, and other verbs sometimes, omitted; in these cases the negative adverb takes the place of a verb and a double negative has the force of an affirmative.

此事不甚要緊 tzĭ szĭ buh shen yao gin, *this matter is not very important.*

In this example the negative adverb 不 buh, *not*, has the force of the verb *is not.*

他報告的信息很不好 ta bao-gao dy hsin-hsih hen buh hao
the news he reported was very bad.

Literally the sentence reads "*The news he reported very was not good,*" i.e., "*was very bad.*" The student must ever keep in mind that we are studying the grammar of the Chinese sentence, not the English translation of that sentence. The verb is 不 buh, *was not*, and it is modified by the adverb 很 hen, *very*, which immediately precedes it.

他這個行爲壞極 ta dje-go hsing-wei hwai gih
this action of his was extremely bad.

壞 hwai, *bad*, is usually an adjective but may also be a verb as in the sentence 你壞了我的事 ni hwai-liao o dy szī, *you have spoiled my affairs.* In the sentence given above 壞 hwai, *bad*, is to be taken as the verb *was bad* and is modified by the adverb 極 gih, *extremely*, which follows it.

司馬牛曰人皆有兄弟我獨無 sze-ma-niu yüeh ren giai yu hsiung-di o duh wu, Sze-ma-niu *said*, "*all men have brothers, I only have not.*"

There are two verbs in this sentence. First, 有 yu, *to have*, which is modified by the adverb 皆 giai, here translated *all* as though it were an adjective qualifying the noun *men*. But this is only because English idiom inverts the order of the words. In the Chinese sentence 皆 giai, is an adverb meaning, *usually*, or, *universally* and it modifies the verb 有 yu which it precedes.

The second verb is 無 wu, which is usually the adverb, *not*, but here, standing alone, it is the verb, *have not* and is modified by the adverb 獨 duh, *only* which precedes it.

子夏曰四海之內皆兄弟也 dzī hsia yüeh szī hai djī nui giai hsiung-di ye, Dzī hsia *said*, "*within the four seas all are brothers.*"

In the preceding sentence we found 皆 giai, to be an adverb modifying the verb 有 yu. Here it functions as a verb and is translated by the English words *all are*.

道也者不可須臾離也 dao ye dje buh ko hsü-yü li ye
the truth may not be abandoned for a moment.

SUBJ. 道也者 *The truth.* PRED. 可離 *may abandon*
ADVBS. 不 須臾 *not, momentarily*

可離非道也 ko li fei dao ye, *what (if it is something that) may be abandoned is not truth.*

The predicate in preceding sentence becomes the subject in this.
SUBJ. 可離 *What may be abandoned.* PRED. 非 (not) *is not*
COMPT. 道也 *truth.*

無論他有病無病 wu-lwen ta yu bing wu bing, *whether he has a sickness or has not a sickness.*

SUBJ. 他 *He.* CONJ. 無論 *whether.* PRED. 有 *has.*

PRED. 無 (not) *has not.* OBJ. 病 *disease*

若細讀此書與自身的進步必不無小助 roh hsi duh tsï shu yü dzï shen dy dzin bu bih buh wu hsiao dzu, *if (you) carefully read this book it will certainly not be without some slight advantage to your personal progress.*

This sentence is worthy of note because it shows how two negatives 不 buh, *not* and 無 wu, *not* or, *without*, form an affirmative verb which is modified by the adverb 必 bih, *certainly* and by a prepositional phrase.

SUBJ. 若細讀此書 *The careful reading of this book*

PRED. 不無 *not without* (will not be without; will have)

ADV. 必 *certainly.* Modifying 不無

OBJ. 小助 *slight advantage.*

PREP. PHRASE 與自身的進步 *to your personal progress.*

美國的開戰决不如中國之毫無預備 mei gwoh dy kai-djan güeh buh ru djung gwoh dj hao wu yü bei, *America's act of war (was) very unlike China's absolute unpreparedness.*

In this example we have again two adverbs which, together, become a verb. The adverbs are 不 buh, *not* and 如 ru, *like*, and these are modified by the preceding adverb 决 güeh, *very*, The two first words 不如 taken together are the equivalent of *unlike.* But 不如 in Chinese is certainly a verb. We must regard it as such though by construing "was unlike" as a verb we do a certain violence to English grammar.

SUBJ. 美國之開戰 *America's act of war*

PRED. 不如 *was unlike.* ADV. 决 *very*

COMP. 中國之毫無預備 *China's absolute unpreparedness*

華人的輿論極不一致 hwa ren dy yü-lwen gih buh ih djï *Chinese opinion (was) extremely lacking in unanimity.*

SUBJ. 華人的輿論 *Chinese opinion.* PRED. 不 (not) *was not*

ADV. 極 *Extremely.* COMP. 一致 *Unanimous*

LESSON XXII.

Sign of the object.

The character 將 dziang, *to take* and its colloquial equivalent 把 ba *to grasp* are said by some writers on Chinese to be "the sign of the object," because they immediately precede the object in the sentence. But these two characters are verbs and they precede the object exactly as other verbs in the active voice do;

it seems therefore simpler and better to construe them in their ordinary sense as active verbs. For example

把門關上 ba men gwan shang, *take the door and shut* (*it*).

他將書讀完 ta dziang shu duh wan, *he took the book and read it through.*

In these sentences two distinct actions are in the mind of the speaker and therefore two verbs are used to express them. The first idea is the mental picture of stretching out the hand and taking hold of the door, the second is the action of closing it. In the second sentence two actions are again present to the mind, first, taking the book, then, reading it. Making a diagram we arrange the parts thus.

SUBJECT.	PREDICATE.	OBJECT
(you)	把	門
,,	關上	(it)
他	將	書
,,	讀完	(it)

If 把 and 將 are construed as "signs of the object" then the verbs 關上 and 讀完 have retrospective action in that the objects 門 and 書 come before the verb, an altogether unusual construction. Moreover in compound sentences the verb would have to be construed as having a principal object preceding it and a supplementary object following it, a construction that seems unnecessarily clumsy.

If the characters 將 and 把 and no others were used in the construction given above it would be right to assign to them a special function as "signs of the object" but when we find that many verbs are used in an identical manner we are compelled either to regard each of those verbs as being a "sign of the object" or else construe 將 and 把 in their primary sense as we do the other verbs. The point will be made clear if we write out a single sentence several times merely altering the verb which occupies the place of the so-called "sign of the object" but not changing the meaning or construction of the sentence.

我將他當好人 o dziang ta dang hao ren, *I took him to be a good man.*

我把他當好人 o ba ta dang hao ren, *I took him to be a good man.*

我以他爲好人 o i ta wei hao ren, *I regarded him as being a good man.*

我認他是好人 o ren ta shī hao ren, *I recognised him as being a good man.*

我當他做好人 o dang ta dzo hao ren, *I esteemed him as being a good man.*

我看他是好人 o kan ta shī hao ren, *I looked on him as being a good man.*

The list of verbs might be extended or any other assertion cast in the same form but these are enough to show that if the first verb in a sentence of this kind is to be construed as "the sign of the object" then the student will find a bewildering number of such "signs" in his reading and he will find it much easier to take the character in its primary and obvious meaning as an active verb.

官長將被拿之人立卽釋放了他 gwan djang dziang bei na djī ren lih dzih shīh-fang liao ta, *the Mandarin took the man who had been arrested and immediately released him.*

兵丁把那些俘擄一齊鎗斃 bing-ding ba na hsie fu-lu ih chi chiang-bi, *the soldiers took the prisoners of war and shot them all.*

Object separated from the verb by Attributive Clauses.

Any number of qualifying clauses may come between the verb and its object. The sentence given above 我以他爲好人 o i ta wei hao ren, *I regarded him as a good man*, may be amplified *at pleasure, e.g.*

我以他爲有道德的好人 o i ta wei yu dao deh dy hao ren *I regarded him as a having-moral-virtue good man.*

The verb is 爲 the qualifying clause is 有道德的好 and so on in the examples following.

我以他爲天下第一有道德的好人 o i ta wei tien hsia di ih yu dao deh dy hao ren, *I regarded him as being the first having-moral-virtue good man in the world.*

我以他爲天下第一有高等道德的好人 o i ta wei tien hsia di ih yu gao deng dao deh dy hao ren, *I regarded him as being the first having exalted moral virtue good man in the world.*

LESSON XXIII.

Adverbial Modifiers.

Adverbial phrase modifiers are numerous. They may either precede or follow the verb but the construction presents no particular difficulty.

他能做完完全全的 ta neng dzo wan wan tsüen tsüen dy *he can do it perfectly and completely.*

The verb is 能做 *can do.* The last five characters form an adverbial phrase.

今晚走得到嗎 gin wan dzou deh dao ma, *shall we arrive there this evening?*

The verb is 走 *walk* the adverb is 得到 *get there.*

這話說不到 dje hwa shwoh buh dao, *these words may not be spoken.*

The verb is 說 *speak* the adverb is 不到 *not get there*, meaning if spoken the "words" will not have the effect intended.

他不知不覺自己吐露出來 ta buh djï buh gioh dzï-gi tu lou chuh lai, *unconsciously he revealed it himself.*

The verb is 吐露出來 (lit, spat it out) the adverb is 不知不覺.

他千方百計東扯西拉總想遮掩 ta chien fang beh gi, dung che hsi la, dzung hsiang dje yen, *with a thousand schemes and a hundred plans, dragging in (irrelevant matter) from the east and west, he earnestly thought to conceal (it.)*

The verb is 想 modified by its adverb 總, the object is 遮掩.

The adverbial modifiers are 千方百計 and 東扯西拉.

The Predicate Adjective.

The predicate adjective is sometimes placed between the two characters forming the verb.

他的臉剃光了 ta dy lien ti gwang liao *his face was shaved clean.*

那個釘子要釘牢了 na-go ding dz gao ding lao liao *that nail must be nailed firm.*

請你把門關緊了 ching ni-ba men gwan gin liao
please shut the door fast.

水罐子倒滿了 shui gwan-dz dao man liao
fill the water jug full.

花瓶擦乾淨了罷 hwa-ping tsah gan-dzing liao ba
polish the vase clean.

The construction in each of the above sentences is the same. The second last character in the line is an adjective; the two characters between which it is placed are the verb. But in the last sentence the character 罷 at the end of the line is the sign of the imperative; (p. 65) the adjective in this sentence is compound, being composed of the two characters 乾淨 gan-dzing, *clean*, which are fourth and fifth in the line.

Demonstrative Adjective.

The numeral 一 ih *one* is used as a demonstrative adjective and placed before some verbs to transform them into nouns.

In the following sentences, which illustrate this construction, the character preceding the numeral is the verb and the character, or characters, immediately following it is the noun.

等一等 deng ih deng, *wait a wait;* the second 等 is a noun.

看一看 kan ih kan, *look a look;* the second 看 is a noun.

坐一坐 dzo ih dzo, *sit down for a moment* (lit. sit a sit).

他笑了一笑 ta hsiao liao ih hsiao, *he laughed a laugh.*

一人不開一開口 ih ren buh kai ih kai kou, *not one man opened his mouth.* 開口 is the noun.

掉挽了一掉挽 diao-hwan liao ih diao hwan, *exchange it (an exchange) for me.*

挪移一挪移 no-i ih no-i, *move it a move.*

排一排坐位一人盡挨得下 pai ih pai dzo wei ih ren dzin ai deh hsia, *arrange the seats a little (an arrangement) and there is plenty of room for one more person.* The 排 following the numeral is the noun.

LESSON XXIV.

Compound Verbs.

A verb may be one, two, three or more characters; when several characters combine to form a verb part of the combination approximates to the function of an adverb. We have seen that adverbs sometimes have verbal force and that the distinction betwixt the adverb and the verb is not always clear.

On page 64 we had the sentence 他的滿面紅漲起來了 ta dy man mien hung chang chi lai liao, *her whole face flushed red*, and noted that the verb consisted of four characters 漲起來了. Now the two middle characters 起來 might be translated by the word "gradually" and so be parsed as an adverb, but if we think only of the Chinese sentence and not of the English translation we shall see that the four characters form one compound verb.

We learned at the commencement of this book that Chinese is a picture language. An action cannot be portrayed by a pictogram as an object like the sun or moon can but the Chinese writer has a tendency to write picturesque phrases as though he were painting word pictures.

In the sentence we are considering the writer tells us of a lady who blushed until her face was suffused red and he pictures the act of blushing in the four characters 漲起來了. Now, each of those characters is itself a verb; 漲 is *to rise* as the water swells imperceptibly with the rising tide; 起 is *to raise up*; 來 is *to come*, and 了 is the verbal particle denoting a finished action.

The whole verb describes how the flush rose up till the whole face was covered by it and depicts a single action correctly described by the English word "flushed."

得福就在椅子上坐了下來 Deh-fuh dziu dzai i-dz shang dzo-liao hsia-lai, *Deh-fuh thereupon sat down on the chair.*

The verb is 坐了下來. Here again 下來 being translated by the word "*down*" might he regarded as an adverb but 下 is a verb as in the combination 下馬 hsia ma, *get off a horse*, or 下樓 hsia lou, *come downstairs*, and the four character verb describes the action of sitting down as the writer saw it.

The following examples are to be construed in the same way.

貞德聽罷也不免心動起來了 Djen-deh ting pa ye buh mien hsin dung chi lai liao. *When Djen-deh had heard all this she could not help her heart being moved.*

The verb is 動起來了

衆人把二位圍將攏來 djung ren ba er wei wei dziang lung lai, *the crowd took and surrounded the two men.*

The verb is 圍將攏來

秀英笑口大張難將嘴合閉攏來 Hsiu-ying hsiao kou da djang nan dziang dzui hoh-pi lung-lai, *Hsiu-ying laughed with her mouth wide open till she found it difficult to bring her lips together again.*

The verb is 合閉攏來

福生皺眉跳起來了 Fuh-seng dzou mei tiao chi lai-liao, *Fuh-seng wrinkled his brows and jumped up.*

The verb is 跳起來了

Numerary Adjuncts.

In Chinese no number is ever expressed without being immediately followed by a numerary adjunct or classifier. These classifiers perform the same office in Chinese as do the words "bar," "blocks" "rolls," in the English phrases "one bar of iron." "Three blocks of stone." "Five rolls of cloth." In English the use of a "classifier" is occasional; in Chinese it is invariable. In English we say "One man." "Ten horses." "Three dogs." In Chinese we must say

一個人 ih go ren, *one* (*piece*) *man.*

十塊墨圓 shih kwai meh yüen, *ten* (*lumps*) *Mexican dollars.*

三條狗 san tiao kou, *three* (*lengths*) *dog.*

The 個 go 塊 kwai and 條 tiao are the classifiers. They are always used thus:—following the number and preceding the noun. A list of the more common of these adjuncts is appended but the table could be greatly extended.

個[4] go. The most common classifier in the language: may be used to precede almost any noun.

塊[4] kwai, *a lump;* classifier of dollars and things that go in chunks, e.g., stones.

本[4] ben, *a root;* classifier of books.

件[4] gien, *an article;* classifier of garments, affairs, etc.

張[1] djang, *a sheet;* classifier of things that go in sheets as, panes of glass, sheets of paper, etc.

位[4] wei, *a dais;* classifier of persons, used in place of 個 go in polite conversation.

把[3] ba, *to grasp;* classifier of things with handles, knives, chairs, ploughs, etc.

隻[1] djï, *one of a pair;* classifier of fowls, boats, etc.

匹[3] pih, *a mate;* classifier of horses.

條[2] tiao, *a length;* classifier of things that go in lengths as thread, drains, etc.

封[1] feng, *to seal;* classifier of letters. An envelope.

句[4] gü, *a sentence;* classifier of sentences.

角[3] gioh, *a corner;* classifier of 10 and 20 cent pieces.

間[1] gien, *a space;* classifier of rooms.

口[3] kou, *the mouth;* classifier of wells, caves, etc.

扇[4] shan, *a fan;* classifier of doors.

雙[1] shwang, *a pair;* classifier of couples. Boots, socks, etc.

疋[3] pih, *a roll;* classifier of pieces of cloth.

層[2] tseng, *a layer;* classifier of steps, stories, etc.

頭[2] tou, *the head;* classifier of oxen, donkeys, etc.

管[3] gwan, *a tube;* classifier of pencils.

DICTIONARY *

Chinese - English

Chinese Grammar Self-taught.

1

一 1 ih
one, unity
one stroke

丁 2 ding
nail, a person

七 1 tsih
seven
two strokes

丈 4 djang
10 feet

三 1 san
three

上 3.4 shang
above, go up

下 4 hsia
below
three strokes

不 1 buh
negative, not

丑 3 djou
1-3 a.m.

丐 4 gai
beggar
four strokes

丘 1 giu
hillock

且 3 chie
moreover

丕 1 pei
great

世 4 shï
the world

丙 3 bing
a stem
five strokes

丞 2 cheng
to aid
seven strokes

並 5 bing
also; moreover

2

丨 kwen
a stroke
two strokes

个 5 go
numerary adjunct
three strokes

中 1 djung
middle

丰 1 feng
graceful
four strokes

丱 4 gwan
tufts of hair
six strokes

串 4 chwan
to string

3

丶 3 dju
a dot

丸 2 wan
a pellet
three strokes

丹 1 dan
carnation
four strokes

主 3 dju
Lord

4

丿 1 pieh
a dash
two strokes

乃 3 nai
but, moreover

久 3 giu
long time
three strokes

之 1 djï
possessive particle
four strokes

乍 4 dja
immediately

乎 1 hu
interrogative

乏 2 fah
to be short of
seven strokes

乘 1 cheng
to ride, avail
nine strokes

乖 2 gwai
strange, uncanny

5

乙 4 ih
used for—one
one stroke

九 3 giu
nine
two strokes

乞 3 chïh
to beg

也 3 ye
also
seven strokes

乳 3 ru
milk, the breasts
ten strokes

乾 1 gan, *dry*
(*also read chien*)
twelve strokes

亂 4 lwan
disorderly

6

亅 güeh
a hook

* *See* Note, *p.* 150.

了[3] liao *final particle*
three strokes
予[2] yü *to give*
seven strokes
事[4] szï *affairs*

7

二[4] er *two*
one stroke
于[2] yü *in, to, at*
two strokes
云[2] yün *to say*
互[4] hu *mutual*
五[3] wu *five*
井[3] ching *a well*
four strokes
亙[4] geng *extreme limit*
five strokes
些[1] hsie *some, a few*
six strokes
亞[4] ya *inferior*
亟[4] gih *hastily*

8

亠 tou *above*
one stroke
亡[2] wang *perished, lost*
four strokes
交[1] giao *intercourse*
亥[4] hai *9-11 p.m.*
亦[4] ih *also*
five strokes
亨[1] heng *prosperous*
six strokes
享[3] hsiang *to enjoy*
京[1] ging *the capital*
seven strokes
亭[2] ting *a rest house*
亮[4] liang *light, clear*
eight strokes
毫[2] hao *point of a hair*

9

人[2] ren *man*
two strokes
什[2] shih *file of ten men*
仁[2] ren *benevolence*
仄[4] dzeh *deflected*
仆[1] puh *a servant*
仇[2] chou *an enemy*
今[1] gin *now, the present*
介[4] giai *between*
仍[2] reng *still, usual*
three strokes
仔[3] dzï *careful*
仕 szï *an official*
他[1] ta *pronoun, he*
仗[4] djang *depend on, fight*
付[4] fu *to deliver to*
仙[1] hsien *an immortal*
同[2]仝 tung *together*
代[4] dai *instead of*
令[4] ling *command, honoured*
以[3] i *accord to*
four strokes
仰[3] yang *to look up*
仲[4] djung *the second*
伙[3] ho *tools*
件[4] gien *numerary of articles*
任[2] ren *a trust, office*
企[4] chi *to stand on tiptoe*
伊[1] i *pronoun, he*
伍[3] wu *file of five men*
伏[2] fuh *to fall down*
伐 fah *to punish*
休[1] hsiu *to desist*
five strokes
伯[4] beh *an uncle*
估[3] gu *to estimate*
伴[4] ban *a companion*
伶[2] ling *clever*
伸[1] shen *to stretch out*
伺[4] tzï *to serve*
似[4] szï *similar*
佃[4] dien *a farmer*
但[4] dan *but*
佈[4] bu *to diffuse*

位[4] wei *a seat*
低[1] di *the bottom*
住[4] dju *to dwell*
佐[3] dzo *to assist*
佑[4] yu *to aid*
佔[4] djan *to usurp*
何[2] ho *why?*
佗[1] toh *humpbacked*
余[2] yü *pronoun, I*
佚[4] ih *leisure*
佛[2] fuh *Buddha*
作[4] dzoh *to do*
佞[4] ning *wordy, specious*
你[3] ni *pronoun, you*

six strokes

佩[4] pei *to hang from the girdle*
佯[2] yang *hypocritical*
佳[1] gia *beautiful, good*
使[3] shï *a messenger*
侃[3] kan *boldly*
來[2] lai *to come*
侈[3] chïh *extravagant*
例[4] li *laws, rules*
侍[4] shï *to wait on*
侔[2] mou *a companion*
供[1] gung *to give*
依[1] i *to trust to*

seven strokes

侮[3] wu *to disgrace*
侯[2] hou *a marquis*
侵[1] chin *to encroach*
侶[3] lu *fellow officials*
便[4] bien *convenient* (read pien, *cheap*)
係[4] hsi *consequences*
促[4] tsuh *to hurry*
俊[4] djün *handsome*
俎[3] dzu *sacrificial vessels*
俗[2] suh *common*
俘[1] fu *prisoner of war*
保[3] bao *to protect*
俟[4] szï *to wait for*
俠[1] giah *a hero*
信[4] hsin *to believe*

eight strokes

修[1] hsiu *to rectify*
俯[3] fu *official residence*
俱[1] chü *all, complete*
傚[4] hsiao *imitate*
俸[4] feng *emolument*
俾[1] bei *to enable, help*
俺[2] an *pronoun, I*
併[4] bing *level with, even*
倉[1] tsang *a granary*
個[4] go *numerary adjunct*
倍[4] bei *double, to add to*
倏[4] shu *hurriedly*
倒[3] dao *upside down*
倡[1] chang *to promote*
倔[2] güeh *sulky*
倖[4] hsing *lucky*
倘[3] tang *if, but*
候[4] hou *to wait*
倚[3] i *to lean against*
借[4] dzie *to borrow*
倣[3] fang *to imitate*
値[2] djïh *value*
倦[4] güen *fatigue*
倫[2] lwen *relations*
倭[1] wo *a dwarf*
們[2] men *plural number*

nine strokes

假[3] gia *to pretend*
偉[2] wei *gigantic*
偺[2] tsa *we*
偏[1] pien *deflected*
偕[1] giai *to accompany*
停[2] ting *to wait*
健[4] gien *strong*

側[4] tseh *at the side of*
偵[1] djeng *a spy*
偶[3] ou *a companion, an idol*
偷[1] tou *to steal*
做[4] dzo *to make*

ten strokes

傅[4] fu *to superintend*
傍[2] pang *side of*
傑[2] gieh *a hero*
傘[3] san *umbrella*
備[4] bei *prepared*
傢[1] gia *tools*

eleven strokes

催[1] tsui *to urge*
傭[2] yung *a servant*
傲[4] ao *proud*
傳[2] chwan *to transmit*
債[4] djai *debt*
傷[1] shang *to injure*
傾[2] ching *to overturn*
僅[4] gin *only*
僇[4] luh *foolish*

twelve strokes

像[4] hsiang *a likeness*
僑[2] chiao *an emigrant*
僕[2] puh *servant, slave*
僚[2] liao *petty official*
僞[4] wei *false, scheming*
僥[2] giao, hsiao *fortunate, chance*
僧[1] seng *bonze*
僭[4] dzien *presume, insult*

thirteen strokes

僵[1] giang *stubborn, stiff*
價[4] gia *price*
僻[4] pih *rustic, vicious*
儀[2] i *ceremony, rites*
儆[3] ging *to warn*
儉[3] gien *economical*

fourteen strokes

儐[4] bin *to entertain*
儒[2] ru *literati*
儕[2] chai *a class, we*
償[2] chang *to repay*
優[1] yu *generous, excellent*
儲[2] chu *to save, bank*

seventeen strokes

10

儿[1] ren *man*

one stroke

允[3] yün *promise*
元[2] yüen *first*

three strokes

兄[2] hsiung *elder brother*
充[1] chung *to fill up*

four strokes

兆[3] djao *an omen*
兇[1] hsiung *fierce*
先[1] hsien *first, before*
光[1] gwang *light, brilliant*

five strokes

克[4] keh *to be able*
兌[4] dui *to exchange*
免[3] mien *to avoid, forgive*

six strokes

兒[2] er *a son*
兎[4] tu *a hare*

nine strokes

兢[2] ging *to strive*

11

入[4] ruh *to enter*

two strokes

內[4] nui *inside*

four strokes

全[2] tsüen *perfectly*

six strokes

兩[3] liang *an ounce*

seven strokes

12

八[1] bah *eight*

two strokes

公[1] gung *public*
六[4] luh *six*

four strokes

共[1] gung *together*

five strokes

兵[1] bing *soldiers*
six strokes
其[2] chi *pronoun, it*
具[4] gü *all, every*
典[3] dien *a law, rule*
eight strokes
兼[1] gien *both*
fourteen strokes
冀[4] gi *to hope for*

13

冂 giung *enclosure*
three strokes
册[4] tseh *account book*
再[4] dzai *again*
seven strokes
冒[4] mao *rash, daring*
冕[3] mien *a crown*

14

冖 mi *a cover*
two strokes
冠[1] gwan *a head-dress*
eight strokes
冥[2] ming *dark, hades*

15

冫 bing *an icicle*
three strokes
冬[1] dung *freezing, winter*
four strokes
冰[1] bing *ice*
冲[1] chung *to dash against*
five strokes
况[4] kwang *moreover*
冶[3] yeh *to melt*
冷[3] leng *cold*
eight strokes
凄[1] tsi *pitiful, cruel*
准[3] djwen *permit*
凉[2] liang *cool*
凋[1] diao *to wither*
凌[2] ling *insult, slice*
凍[4] dung *freeze*
nine strokes
減[3] gien *reduce*
thirteen strokes
凜[3] ling *awe, shiver*
凝[2] ning *to congeal*

16

几[1] gi *a stool*
one stroke
凡[2] fan *all*
nine strokes
凰[2] hwang *phoenix*
ten strokes
凱[1] kai *victory*
凳[4] deng *a stool*

17

凵 kan *to contain*
凶[1] hsiung *wicked*
three strokes
凸[4] du *to protrude*
凹[1] wa *concave*
出[1] chuh *come out*
six strokes
函[2] han *a letter*

18

刀[1] dao *a knife*
one stroke
刁[1] diao *crafty*
刃[4] ren *an edge*
two strokes
分[1] fen *a part, divide*
切[4] chieh *to slice, a slice*
three strokes
刊[1] kan *cut, engrave*
four strokes
刑[2] hsing *to punish*
列[4] lieh *arrange in order*
five strokes
初[1] chu *the beginning*
删[1] shan *to excise*
判[4] pan *to punish*
別[2] bieh *to separate*
利[4] li *profit*
six strokes
刮[1] gwah *to scrape*
到[4] dao *arrive, reach to*
制[4] djï *govern, arrange*

刷[1] shwah *a brush, to brush*
券[4] chüen *a roll, book*
刺[4] tzï *prick, a thorn*
刻[4] keh *engrave, moment*

seven strokes

則[2] dzeh *thereupon, then*
削[1] hsioh *to pare*
剋[4] keh *destroy, cut out*
前[2] chien *before, formerly*

eight strokes

剖[3] pou *split, open*
剛[1] gang *steel*
剝[1] boh *to strip*

nine strokes

剪[3] gien *scissors*
副[4] fu *aid, a deputy*
剩[4] sheng *a surplus*

ten strokes

割[1] goh *to cut*
創[4] chwang *to carve, make*

eleven strokes

剿[3] dziao *to exterminate*
劍[4] gien *a sword*
劈[1] pih *to split*

fourteen strokes

劑[4] dzi *dose of medicine*

19

力[4] lih *strength*

three strokes

功[1] gung *labour, merit*
加[2] gia *to add*

four strokes

劣[4] lieh *inferior*

five strokes

助[4] dzu *to assist*
努[3] nu *violent, strong*
効[4] hsiao *to toil*

six strokes

勁[4] ging *strong*
勃[4] poh *suddenly*
勅[4]敕 chïh *command*
勇[3] yung *brave, a soldier*
勉[3] mien *to urge*

eight strokes

勒[4] leh *to restrain*
動[4] dung *to move*
勘[4] kan *investigate*
務[4] wu *business, must*

ten strokes

勳[1] hsün *meritorious*
勝[1] sheng *to overcome*
勞[2] lao *labour*

eleven strokes

募[4] mo *to enrol*
勢[4] shï *power, force*
勤[2] chin *diligence*

fourteen strokes

勵[4] li *stimulate*
勸[4] chüen *to exhort*

20

勹 pao *to wrap*

one stroke

勺[2] shoh *a spoon*

two strokes

勻[2] yün *even, equal*
勾[1] gou *a hook*
勿[4] wuh *do not*

three strokes

包[1] bao *to wrap, a bundle*

nine strokes

匍[2] pu *to crawl*
匐[4] fuh *to creep*

21

匕 bi a spoon

two strokes

化[4] hwa *transform, influence*

three strokes

北[3] beh *North*

nine strokes

匙[2] chï *a spoon, key*

22

匚 fang *a chest*

three strokes

匝[1] dzah *circle, wheel*

four strokes

匠[4] dziang *a workman*
匡[1] kwang *a box*

匣4 hsiah
a casket
eight strokes
匪3 fei
a criminal, negative
eleven strokes
匯3 hwei
whirlpool, bank draft
匱4 guei
cupboard

23

匸 hsi
to conceal
two strokes
匹3 pih
numerary adjunct, a pair
nine strokes
匾3 bien
a signboard
匿4 nih
to hide

24

十2 shïh
ten
one stroke
千1 chien
one thousand
two strokes
升1 sheng
to ascend, a pint
午3 wu
11-1 o'clock noon
three strokes
卉4 hwei
flowers
半4 ban
a half
six strokes
卑1 bei
low, humble
卒2 dzuh
lictors, the end
卓1 djoh
great
協2 hsieh
to co-operate
seven strokes
南2 nan
South
ten strokes
博4 boh
expansive, a scholar

25

卜3 buh
to divine
three strokes
占1 djan
to foretell
five strokes
卦4 gwa
diagram

26

卩 dzieh
a joint
卯3 mao
5-7 a.m.
four strokes
印4 yin
to print
危1 wei
dangerous
five strokes
卵3 lwan
eggs
six strokes
卷4 güen
scroll, book
卸4 hsie
to unload
卹4 hsüh
compassionate
seven strokes
即2 dzih
thereupon
卻4 chioh
but, to decline
卿1 ching
a statesman

27

厂 han
a cliff
厓1 gwei
sceptre
seven strokes
厚4 hou
thick, generous
eight strokes
原2 yüen
origin
厠4 szï
a privy
厦4 hsia
a mansion
twelve strokes
厭4 yen
to dislike

28

厶 szï
private, selfish
three strokes
去4 chü
to go away
nine strokes
參1 tsan
to assist, consult

29

又4 yu
again, also
two strokes
及2 gih
to reach to
友3 yu
a friend
反3 fan
to reverse
six strokes
取3 chü
to choose, take
受4 shou
to receive
seven strokes
敘4 hsü
to talk

叛4 pan *to rebel*

sixteen strokes

叢2 tsung *crowded*

30

口3 kou *a mouth*

two strokes

古3 gu *ancient*

句4 gü *a sentence*

叨1 tao *addicted to*

叩4 kou *to rap, knock*

只3 djï *only, but*

叫4 giao *to call*

召4 djao *to call*

可3 ko *may, can*

台2 tai *eminent*

史3 shï *history*

右4 yu *the right side*

司1 szï *officer, to manage*

另4 ling *beside, extra*

three strokes

吃1 chïh *to eat*

各4 goh *each, every*

合2 hoh *united, together*

吉2 gih *lucky*

同2 tung *together*

名2 ming *a name*

后4 hou *Empress*

吏4 li *a petty official*

吊4 diao *suspend*

吐4 tu *to vomit*

向4 hsiang *towards*

four strokes

君1 gün *prince, superior*

吝4 lin *stingy, miserly*

吞1 tun *to swallow*

否3 fou *negative, not*

含2 han *to hold in the mouth*

吩1 fen *to order*

呈2 cheng *to present, report*

吳2 wu *a surname*

吸1 hsih *to in-breathe*

吹1 chui *to blow breath*

吼3 hou *to growl*

吾2 wu *pronoun, I*

告4 gao *to tell*

five strokes

周2 djou *a circle*

味4 wei *taste*

呼1 hu *call, exhale*

呢1 ni *interrogative*

呪4 djou *charm, curse*

咐4 fu *to order*

命4 ming *life, fate*

和2 ho *harmony, peaceful*

咎4 giu *a fault*

six strokes

咫3 djï *near, a foot*

咬3 yao *to bite*

咸2 hsien *all, together*

咽4 yen *to swallow*

哀1 ai *pitiful*

品3 pin *class*

哄3 hung *coax, cheat*

哇1 wa *to cry*

哉1 dzai *an exclamation*

咳2 keh *cough*

seven strokes

員2 yüen *an official, delegate*

哥1 go *elder brother*

哭1 kuh *cry, weep*

哲4 djeh *wise*

唆1 so *to incite*

唇2 chwen *the lips*

唐2 tang *tang dynasty*

售4 shou *to sell*

唱4 chang *to sing*

唾4 tu *to spit*

商2 shang *a merchant*

問4 wen
to ask
啟3 chi
to open
nine strokes
啼2 ti
to cry, weep
善3 shan
good, virtuous
喊3 han
to call out
喚4 huan
to call
喜3 hsi
pleasure
喉2 hou
throat
喻4 yü
metaphor
喝1 hoh
to drink
喧1 hsüen
clamour
喫1 chïh
to eat
喪1 sang
to mourn, lose
單1 dan
a unit, single
ten strokes
嗎1 ma
interrogative
嗇4 seh
miserly
嗣4 szï
afterwards, posterity
嗤1 chï
to laugh
eleven strokes
嘆4 tan
to sigh
嘉1 gia
elegant
嘗2 chang
to taste
嘔1 ou
to vomit
嘿4 meh
silently
器4 chi
a vessel, dish
嘴3 dzui
lips
sixteen strokes
嚮4 hsiang
towards
seventeen strokes
嚴2 yen
severe
嚼4 dzioh
to chew
nineteen strokes
囊 nang
a bag
twenty-two strokes
囑3 djuh
to command

31

囗 wei
an enclosure
two strokes
囚2 chiu
a prisoner
四4 szï
four
four strokes
回2 hwei
revolve, return
因1 yin
because
困4 kwen
bind, a bundle
five strokes
固4 gu
firm, determined
eight strokes
圈4 chüen
a ring, circle
國2 gwoh
kingdom
nine strokes
圍2 wei
to surround
ten strokes
園2 yüen
a garden
圓2 yüen
round
eleven strokes
圖2 tu
a plan, map
團2 twan
a ball, round

32

土3 tu
earth, mud
three strokes
在4 dzai
to be, there, at
圭1 gwei
a sceptre
地4 di
the earth
four strokes
址3 djï
a foundation
均1 gün
even, equal
坊1 fang
a place, lane
坎3 kan
a pit, hole
坏1 pi
a mud brick
坐4 dzo
a seat
坑1 keng
a ditch
five strokes
坡1 po
a bank
坤1 kwen
the earth
坦3 tan
level
垂2 chui
to hang down
six strokes
型2 hsing
to mould
垢4 gou
dust, dirt
垣2 yüen
a wall
埃2 ai
dust
埋2 mai
to bury
城2 cheng
a city
eight strokes

域[4] yüh
a region
執[2] djïh
to seize
培[2] pei
add earth to
基[1] gi
foundation
堂[2] tang
a hall
堅[1] gien
firm, secure
堆[2] dui
a heap
nine strokes
堡[3] bao
a fortress
堤[1] di
an embankment
堦[1] giai
steps
堪[1] kan
to sustain
堯[2] yao
an Emperor
報[4] bao
to report, newspaper
堵[3] du
to stop up
ten strokes
塊[4] kwai
a lump
塑[4] su
to mould, model
塔[3] tah
a pagoda
塗[2] tu
smear with mud
塚[3] djung
a mound, grave
塞[4] seh
to stop up
塡[2] tien
to fill up
塢[3] wu
a dock
塌[1] tah
to depress
eleven strokes
塲[2] chang
an open space
塵[2] chen
dust
塾[2] shuh
a school
境[4] ging
a boundary
墊[4] dien
fill up
墓[4] mo
a grave
twelve strokes
墜[4] djui
to fall down
增[1] dzeng
to add to
墨[4] meh
ink
墩[1] dun
a mound
墮[4] do
to fall down
墳[2] fen
a grave
thirteen strokes
墾[3] ken
to break new soil
壁[4] bih
partition wall
壇[2] tan
an altar
fourteen strokes
壓[1] yah
to repress
fifteen strokes
壘[3] lei
piled up
sixteen strokes
壞[4] hwai
spoiled
壟[3] lung
a hillock
seventeen strokes
壤[3] rang
loam

33

士[4] szï
a scholar
one stroke
壬[2] ren
ninth of the ten stems
four strokes
壯[4] djwang
strong
eight strokes
壺[2] hu
a pot
nine strokes
壻[4] hsü
a son-in-law
eleven strokes
壽[4] shou
longevity

34

夂 djïh
to step

35

夊 tsui
step slowly
夏 hsia
summer

36

夕[1] hsih
evening
two strokes
外[4] wai
outside
three strokes
夙[4] suh
early morning
多[1] do
many
five strokes
夜[4] ye
night
eleven strokes
夢[4] meng
a dream
夥[3] ho
many

37

大[4] da
great
one stroke

天[1] tien *heaven*
太[4] tai *very*
夫[1] fu *a husband*
夭[1] yao *young, calamity*

two strokes

央[2] yang *middle*
失[4] shïh *to lose*

three strokes

夷[2] i *barbarian, easy*

four strokes

夾[1] giah *to nip, double*

five strokes

奄[3] yen *remain, anon*
奇[2] chi *strange*
奈[4] nai *but*
奉[3] feng *to offer*

six strokes

奎[2] kwei *name of a star*
奏[4] dzou *report to the throne*
奔[1] ben *to run*

seven strokes

套[4] tao *to slip on, wear*
奚[1] hsi *why*

nine strokes

奠[4] dien *libation*
奢[1] she *extravagant*

ten strokes

奧[4] ao *mysterious*

eleven strokes

奩[2] lien *toilet box*
奪[2] doh *to snatch*
奬[3] dziang *reward, praise*

twelve strokes

奮[3] fen *to exert*

38

女[3] nü *woman, daughter*

two strokes

奴[2] nu *a slave*
奶[3] nai *milk, breast*

three strokes

奸[1] gien *treacherous*
好[3] hao *good*
如[2] ru *like*
妃[1] fei *imperial concubine*
妄[4] wang *false, reckless*

four strokes

妊[4] ren *pregnant*
妒[4] tu *jealous*
妓[4] gi *a prostitute*
妖[1] yao *imp, fiend*
妙[4] miao *wonderful*
妝[1] djwang *to dress, feign*
妣[3] bi *deceased mother*
妥[3] to *firm, satisfactory*
妨[1] fang *a hindrance*

five strokes

妹[4] mei *younger sister*
妻[1] tsi *wife*
妾[4] tsieh *a concubine*
姊[3] dzï *elder sister*
妯[2] djou *brother's wife*
始[3] shï *the first*
姐[3] dzie *elder sister*
姑[1] gu *an aunt*
姒[3] szï *brother's wife*
姓[4] hsing *name*
委[3] wei *to depute*

six strokes

姚[2] yao *slender*
姜[1] giang *a wild tribe*
姣[3] giao *handsome*
姤[4] kou *to pair*
姦[1] gien *fornication*
姨[2] i *an aunt*
姪[2] djïh *a nephew*
娃[1] wa *baby*
姻[1] yin *bride, marriage*
姿[1] dzï *mien, beauty*
威[1] wei *imposing*

seven strokes

娌[3] li *brother's wife*
娘[2] niang *mother*
娠[1] djen *pregnant*

eight strokes

娶[4] tsü *to take a wife*
娼[1] chang *a prostitute*
婆[2] po *mother-in-law*
婉[3] wan *docile, yielding*
婚[1] hwen *marriage, a bridegroom*
婢[4] bei *female servant*
婦[4] fu *a woman, wife*
婪[2] lan *lewd, covetous*

nine strokes

婿[4] hsü *son-in-law*
媒[2] mei *go-between*
媚[4] mei *to flatter*
媛[2] yüen *a beauty*
媧[1] wa *a mythical woman*

ten strokes

嫁[4] gia *to marry a husband*
嫂[3] sao *elder brother's wife*
嫉[1] dzih *envy*
嫌[2] hsien *to dislike*

eleven strokes

嫡[2] dih *a wife*
嫩[4] nwen *tender*
嫖[2] piao *frequent a brothel*

twelve strokes

嬉[1] hsi *to play*
嬌[1] giao *delicate*
嬖[4] bih *a favourite*

fourteen strokes

嬪[1] bin *a concubine*
嬰[1] ying *an infant*
嬭[3] nai *breasts, milk*

fifteen strokes

嬸[3] shen *an aunt*
孀[1] shwang *a widow*

nineteen strokes

孌[3] lüen *beautiful*

39

子[3] dzï *son*
孑[2] gieh *solitary*

one stroke

孔[3] kung *an orifice, Confucius*

two strokes

孕[4] yün *pregnant*

three strokes

字[4] dzï *Chinese characters*
存[1] tswen *preserve, retain*

four strokes

孚[1] fu *to trust*
孜[1] dzï *diligent*
孝[4] hsiao *filial*

five strokes

孟[4] meng *a name, Mencius*
季[4] gi *a season*
孤[1] gu *an orphan*
孥[2] nu *a child*

six strokes

孩[2] hai *a child*

seven strokes

孫[1] swen *a grandson*

eight strokes

孰[2] shuh *who*

thirteen strokes

學[2] hsioh *a school, study*

fourteen strokes

孺[4] ru *a suckling*

seventeen strokes

孽[4] nieh *consequence of sin*

40

宀 mien *a cover*

two strokes

宅[2] dzah *house, dwelling*

three strokes

守[3] shou *to guard*
安[1] an *peace*

four strokes

宋[4] sung *the Sung Dynasty*
完[2] wan *finished*
宏[2] hung *great, wide*

five strokes

宗[1] tsung *ancestral*
官[1] gwan *a mandarin*
宙[4] djou *the universe*
定[4] ding *fixed*
宛[3] wan *yielding*

宜[2] i
fitting
six strokes
客[4] keh
a guest
宣[1] hsüen
proclaim
室[4] shïh
a house
宥[4] yu
to forgive
宦[4] hwan
officials
宮[1] gung
palace
宰[3] dzai
governor
害[4] hai
to injure
宴[4] yen
a feast
宵[1] hsiao
night
家[1] gia
home
容[2] yung
the countenance
to contain
eight strokes
宿[4] suh
to lodge
寂[4] dzih
still, lonely
寃[1] yüen
grievance
寄[4] gi
to send
寅[2] yin
3 to 5 a.m.
密[4] mih
secret
寇[4] kou
a robber
nine strokes
富[4] fu
wealthy
寐[4] mei
to sleep
寒[2] han
cold
寓[4] yü
a lodging

寔[2] shïh
solid, true
甯[2] ning
peaceful
eleven strokes
寞[4] moh
silent, still
察[2] chah
examine
寡[3] gwa
widow
寢[3] chin
to sleep
寤[4] wu
to be awake
寥[2] liao
empty, wide
實[4] shïh
solid, truth
寧[2] ning
peaceful
twelve strokes
審[3] shen
to examine, judge
寫[3] hsie
to write
寬[1] kwan
broad, forgiving
寮[2] liao
officials
thirteen strokes
寰[2] hwan
palace, the world
sixteen strokes
寵[3] chung
be partial to
seventeen strokes
寶[3] bao
precious

41

寸[4] tswen
an inch
three strokes
寺[4] szï
monastery
six strokes
封[1] feng
to appoint
seven strokes

射[4] she
archery
尅[4] keh
to overcome
eight strokes
將[1] dziang
to take, about to
專[1] djwan
specially
nine strokes
尊[1] dzwen
honourable
尋[2] hsün
to seek
twelve strokes
對[4] dui
opposite
thirteen strokes
導[4] dao
to lead

42

小[3] hsiao
small
one stroke
少[3] shao
few
three strokes
尖[1] gien
a point
尙[4] shang
still, moreover

43

尢[1] wang
bent, lame
尤[2] yu
still more
nine strokes
就[4] dziu
thereupon

44

尸[1] shï
a corpse
one stroke
尹[3] yin
a governor
尺[3] chïh
a foot
two strokes

尼 2 ni *a nun*

four strokes

尾 3 wei *a tail*

尿 4 niao *urine*

局 2 güh *an office*

five strokes

居 1 gü *to dwell*

届 4 giai *a set time*

屈 1 chüh *to stoop, injustice*

six strokes

屋 1 wuh *a house*

屍 1 shï *a corpse*

seven strokes

屐 4 gi *wooden slippers*

屑 4 hsioh *fragments*

展 3 djan *to open*

eight strokes

屏 2 ping *a screen, to reject*

屠 2 tu *to kill*

eleven strokes

屢 3 lü *frequently*

屣 3 hsi *sandals*

twelve strokes

層 2 tseng *a storey, a layer*

履 3 li *shoes, to tread*

eighteen strokes

屬 3 shuh *to belong to*

45

屯 2 tun *collect together*

46

山 1 shan *a hill*

five strokes

岡 1 gang *hilly, a ridge*

岸 4 an *a bank, shore*

岳 4 yoh *hill, father-in-law*

峙 4 chï *peaks*

seven strokes

峰 1 feng *high peak*

島 3 dao *an island*

峽 2 hsiah *a pass*

eight strokes

崇 2 chung *lofty, eminent*

崖 2 yai *steep bank*

崩 1 beng *landslip, death of emperor*

nine strokes

嵌 4 chien *to inlay*

ten strokes

嵩 1 sung *a famous hill*

嶺 3 ling *mountain*

嶽 4 yoh *famous mountain*

47

川 1 chwan *streams*

州 1 djou *divided streams*

巡 2 hsün *to patrol*

巢 2 chao *a nest*

48

工 1 kung *labour*

左 3 dzo *assist*

巧 3 chiao *dexterous*

巫 2 wu *a wizard*

差 1 {cha, *an error*; chai, *send, dispatch*

49

己 3 gi *self*

已 3 i *already*

巳 4 szï *9-11 a.m.*

巴 1 ba *a slap*

巷 4 hsiang *an alley*

50

巾 1 gin *a napkin*

two strokes

市 4 shï *a market*

布 4 bu *cloth*

three strokes

帆 2 fan *a sail*

four strokes

希 1 hsi *strange, wonderful*

five strokes

帑 2 tang *treasury*

帕 4 pa *a veil*

帖 1 tieh *a placard, a bill*

帮 1 bang *to help*

six strokes

帝 4 di *a ruler*
帥 4 shwai *a commander*

seven strokes

師 1 szï *a teacher, master*
席 2 hsih *seat, feast*

eight strokes

帳 4 djang *curtains*
帶 4 dai *to carry*
帷 2 wei *a curtain*
常 2 chang *constantly*

nine strokes

帽 4 mao *a cap*

eleven strokes

幔 4 man *a curtain*
幕 4 mo *a tent*
幗 1 gwoh *apron, women*
幫 1 bang *help*

twelve strokes

幣 4 bi *notes, currency*

51

干 gan *a pole*
平 2 ping *level*
年 2 nien *a year*
并 4 bing *equal*
幸 4 hsing *lucky*
幹 4 gan *trunk, to manage*

52

幺 yao *immature*
幻 4 hwan *mysterious*
幼 4 yu *young*
幽 1 yu *dark*
幾 1 {gi, *a few* / gi3, *how many?*}

53

广 yen *a shelter*

four strokes

庇 4 bi *overshadow*
床 2 chwang *a bed*
序 4 hsü *series, preface*
底 4 di *the bottom*

five strokes

店 4 dien *an inn*
庚 1 geng *seventh stem*
府 3 fu *official residence*

six strokes

庠 2 hsiang *a school*
度 4 du *a measure*

seven strokes

座 4 dzo *a seat*
庫 4 ku *a treasury*
庭 2 ting *a mansion*

eight strokes

庵 1 an *a monastery*
庶 4 shu *many, nearly*
康 2 kang *robust*
庸 2 yung *to use, merit*

nine strokes

廂 1 hsiang *side room*

ten strokes

廉 2 lien *cheap*
廊 2 lang *a porch*

eleven strokes

廚 2 chu *kitchen*
廟 4 miao *a temple*
廠 3 chang *a factory*
廢 4 fei *to abrogate*
廣 3 gwang *wide*

thirteen strokes

廩 3 lin *a granary*

twenty-two strokes

廳 1 ting *a hall, court*

54

廴 yin *motion*
延 2 yen *long*
廷 2 ting *a palace*
建 4 gien *build, robust*
廻 2 hwei *to return, revolve*

55

廾 gung *clasped hands*
弄 4 lung *fondle, play with*
弊 4 bi *fraud*

56

弋^{4} ih *a dart, shoot*

式^{4} shï *a pattern*

弒^{4} shï *to murder*

57

弓^{1} gung *a bow*

one stroke

弔^{4} diao *to suspend, condole*

引^{3} in *to lead*

two strokes

弘^{2} hung *great*

弗^{2} fuh *negative, not*

three strokes

弟^{4} di *younger brother*

five strokes

弩^{3} nu *a bow, strong*

six strokes

弭^{3} mi *repress, stop*

seven strokes

弱^{4} roh *weak*

eight strokes

張^{1} djang *to expand*

强^{2} chiang *strong, violent*

彀^{4} gou *enough*

彈^{1} dan, *crossbow, bullet*; tan^{2}, *to thrum*

fourteen strokes

彌^{2} mi *universal*

彎^{1} wan *a bend*

58

彐 chi *pig's snout*

彙^{4} hui *a compendium*

59

彡 shan *flowing hair*

形^{2} hsing *form, appearance*

彩^{3} tsai *variegated*

彰^{1} djang *brilliant, feathers*

影^{3} ying *a shadow*

60

彳 chïh *to step*

four strokes

彷^{3} fang *like, to imitate*

役^{4} ih *lictors*

five strokes

彿^{4} fuh *resemble*

彼^{3} bi *him, that, the other*

往^{3} wang *go towards*

征^{1} djeng *punitive*

six strokes

待^{4} dai *to wait for*

徇^{2} hsün *to follow*

很^{3} hen *very, intense*

律^{4} lüh *law, rule*

後^{4} hou *afterwards*

seven strokes

徑^{4} ging *a side path*

徒^{2} tu *to follow, a disciple*

eight strokes

得^{2} deh *to obtain*

徙^{3} hsi *remove*

從^{2} tsung *to follow*

御^{4} yü *imperial*

nine strokes

徧^{4} bien *everywhere*

復^{4} fuh *again, repeat*

循^{2} hsün *follow*

ten strokes

微^{2} wei *minute, an atom*

twelve strokes

徵^{1} djeng *to levy, witness*

德^{2} deh *virtue*

徹^{4} cheh *to penetrate*

thirteen strokes

徽^{1} hwui *urgent, elegant*

61

心^{1} hsin *the heart*

one stroke

必^{4} bih *must*

two strokes

忌^{4} gi *jealous*

忍^{3} ren *to endure*

志^{4} djï *resolution*

忘^{2} wang *to forget*

忙^{2} mang *busy*

four strokes

忠1 djung *loyal*
快4 kwai *quick, happy*
念4 nien *to think, read*
忽1 huh *suddenly, to forget*
忿4 fen *anger*

five strokes

怒4 nu *anger*
怕4 pa *to fear*
怙4 hu *presume, obstinate*
思1 szï *to think*
怠4 dai *careless, remiss*
怡2 i *pleasant*
急2 gih *hurried, anxious*
性4 hsing *disposition*
怨4 yüen *grievance, to murmur*
怪4 gwai *strange, uncanny*
怯2 chieh *to be afraid*
怱1 tsung *hurried*
怎3 dzen *why, how*

six strokes

恆2 heng *unchanging*
恊2 hsien *to co-operate*
恃4 shï *to rely on*
恐3 kung *startled, perhaps*
恕4 shu *to forgive*
恙4 yang *sickness*
恢1 hwei *extensive*
恤4 hsüh *compassion*
恨4 hen *to hate, very*
恥3 chï *modesty, shame*
恩1 en *grace, favour*
恪4 keh *sincerity*
恬2 tien *peace*
恭1 gung *respectful*
息2 hsih *rest, to cease*
恰4 chiah *luckily*

seven strokes

悄3 chiao *secretly, quietly*
悅4 yüeh *to be pleased*
悉4 hsih *minute, all*
悌4 di *brotherly love*
悍4 han *obstinate*
悔3 hwei *to repent*
悖4 bei *rebellious*
悞4 wu *neglect, delay*
悟4 wu *awake, discern*
患4 hwan *calamity*
您2 nin *you*

eight strokes

悲1 bei *pitiful, kind*
悶4 men *smother, depress*
悼4 dao *sorrow, sympathy*
悽1 tsi *cruel, pitiful*
情2 ching *affection, appearance*
惑4 hwoh *suspect, delude*
惜1 hsih *alas! pity*
惟2 wei *only, but*
惠4 hwei *kindness, favour*
惡4 { oh, *evil* / wu4, *to dislike* }

nine strokes

惰4 do *lazy*
惱3 nao *to anger*
想3 hsiang *to think*
惶2 hwang *terror*
惹3 rê *to provoke*
惻4 tseh *compassion*
愁2 tsou *grief*
愆1 chien *transgression*
愈4 yü *more, better*
愎4 bih *stubborn*
意4 i *a thought, idea*
愚2 yü *foolish*
愛4 ai *love*
感4 gan *to influence*

ten strokes

愧4 kuei *ashamed*
慎4 shen *careful*
慄4 lih *afraid*

慈 2 tzī *compassionate*
慊 3 chien *to regret, deficient*
態 4 tai *appearance*

eleven strokes

慕 4 mo *to love*
慘 3 tsan *grieved, pain*
慚 2 tsan *ashamed*
慟 4 dung *grieved*
慢 4 man *impolite, slow*
慣 4 gwan *accustomed*
慧 4 hwei *wise, wisdom*
慨 4 gai *affected*
慮 4 lü *anxiety*
慰 4 wei *to comfort*
慶 4 ching *to congratulate*
慷 3 kang *magnanimously*
慾 4 yüh *lust, passion*
憂 1 yu *sorrow*
憎 1 dzeng *to dislike*
憐 2 lien *pity, kind*
憑 2 ping *evidence*
憤 4 fen *exasperation*
憫 3 min *pity, to feel for*
憲 4 hsien *constitution, law*

thirteen strokes

憶 4 i *to recollect*
懂 3 dung *to understand*
懃 2 chin *diligent*
懇 3 keng *to beseech*
懈 4 hsiai *lazy*
應 2 ying *to promise, ought*
懊 4 ao *to regret, vexed*

fifteen strokes

懲 1 cheng *to punish*

sixteen strokes

懶 3 lan *lazy*
懷 2 hwai *affection, think of*

seventeen strokes

懸 2 hsüen *to suspend*

eighteen strokes

懼 4 gü *to fear*
懽 1 hwan *to be pleased*
懿 4 i *dignified*

nineteen strokes

戀 4 lien *to hanker after*

62

戈 1 go *a spear*

one stroke

成 2 cheng *a city*
我 3 o *pronoun, I*
戒 4 giai *to warn, threaten*

four strokes

或 4 hwoh *whether, perhaps*

seven strokes

戚 2 chih *relatives*

eight strokes

戮 4 luh *to slaughter*

twelve strokes

戰 4 djan *to fight, war*
戲 4 hsi *a play*

fourteen strokes

戴 4 dai *wear on the head*

63

戶 4 hu *a door*
戾 4 li *calamity*
房 2 fang *a house*
所 3 so *a place*
扁 3 bien *flat, a tablet*
扇 4 shan *a half door*

64

手 3 shou *a hand*
才 2 tsai *ability*

two strokes

扑 4 puh *to strike*
打 3 da *to hit*
扔 3 reng *throw away*

three strokes

扛 1 kang *to carry*
扞 4 gan *ward off*
托 4 toh *carry on palm*
扣 4 kou *knock, rap*

four strokes

扮 4 ban *to dress, personate*

扶[2] fu *to support*
批[1] pi *to criticise*
承[2] chen *to manage*
技[4] gi *ability*
抄[1] chao *to copy*
扭[3] niu *to twist*
找[3] djao *to find*
把[3] ba *to take*
抑[4] ih *repress, or*
投[2] tou *cast oneself upon*
抗[4] kang *carry*
折[2] djeh *break*
抛[1] pao *cast away*

five strokes

披[1] pi *to wrap*
抱[4] bao *embrace*
抵[3] di *to oppose*
抹[4] moh *to wipe*
押[4] yah *to hold down*
抽[1] chou *to wind*
拂[2] fuh *to repel*
拄[3] dju *to support*
拆[4] cheh *to break*
拇[3] mu *the thumb*
拉[3] la *to drag*
拌[1] ban *to mix*
拏[2] na *to take*
拍[4] peh *to pat*
拒[4] gü *push away*
拐[3] guai *to kidnap*
拈[1] nien *to pick up*
拓[4] toh *a fathom*
拔[4] bah *pluck up*
托[2] toh *to entrust*
拗[3] ao *twisted*
拘[1] gü *to seize*
拙[5] güeh *stupid*
拚[4] pin *to risk*
招[1] djao *to beckon*
拜[4] bai *to worship*

six strokes

括[4] gwah *a slap*
拭[4] shï *to wipe*
拯[3] djeng *lift, save*
拱[3] gung *fold the hands*
拳[1] chüen *the fist*
拾[2] shïh *to pick up*
拿[2] na *to take*
持[2] chï *to hold*
指[3] djï *finger, to point*
按[4] an *to hold down, according to*
挖[1] wah *excavate*
挑[1] tiao *to carry*

seven strokes

挨[1] ai *next to*
挫[4] tso *to repress*
振[4] djen *lift up*
挺[3] ting *stick out*
捆[3] kwen *bind*
捉[4] djoh *catch, seize*
捐[1] güen *contribute*
捕[4] bu *seize, apprehend*
挪[2] no *to move*
挽[3] wan *draw, lead*
捧[3] peng *to hold in both hands*
捨[3] she *relinquish*
捫[1] men *to touch*
捲[3] güen *to roll up*
掀[1] hsien *to uncover*
掃[3] sao *to sweep*
授[4] shou *to give*
掉[4] diao *to fall down*
掌[3] djang *the palm*
掐[1] chiah *grasp*
排[2] pai *spread out*
掘[4] güeh *to dig*
掛[4] gwa *to hang up*
掠[4] lioh *to rob*

採[3] tsai *to pluck*
探[1] tan *feel for, spy*
接[4] dzieh *receive, welcome*
控[4] kung *attack, accuse*
推[1] tui *to push*
掩[3] yen *cover, hide*
措[4] tsoh *arrange*

nine strokes

揀[3] gien *to select*
揆[3] kwei *weigh in the hand*
揉[2] rou *to rub*
描[2] miao *to draw*
提[2] ti *to lift up*
揑[4] nieh *fabricate*
插[4] chiah *stick in ground*
揚[2] yang *scatter*
換[4] hwan *to exchange*
拚[3] ban *challenge, dare*
握[4] wuh *a handful*
揣[3] chwai *think of*
援[1] yüen *assist*
揮[1] hui *throw away*
揭[4] gieh *open*

ten strokes

損[3] sun *to injure*
搓[1] tso *rub in hands*
搔[1] sao *to scratch*
搖[2] yao *to shake*
搗[3] dao *to pound*
搜[1] sou *search*
搶[3] chiang *to rob, violence*
搬[1] ban *to remove*
搯[1] tao *draw out*

eleven strokes

摘[2] dzeh *to pluck*
摟[2] lou *to embrace*
摩[2] mo *to feel for*
摶[2] twan *make a ball*
摸[1] mo *grope, feel for*
摹[2] mo *trace, copy*
摺[4] djeh *to fold*

twelve strokes

撈[2] lao *to rake up*
撐[1] tseng *prop up*
撓[3] naö *scratch, worry*
撕[1] szï *to tear*
撚[3] nien *to twist*
撞[4] djwang *bump against*
撤[4] cheh *take away*
撥[2] boh *empty out*
撫[3] fu *support*
播[4] bo *scatter, sow*
撮[4] tsoh *select*
撰[4] djwan *choose*
撲[2] puh *to strike*
撒[1] sah *to loose*

thirteen strokes

擄[3] lo *carry off*
擇[4] dzeh *choose*
擊[4] gih *strike*
擋[3] dang *oppose*
操[1] tsao *grasp, drill*
擒[2] chin *capture*
擔[3] dan *to bear*
擘[5] boh *to break*
據[4] gü *hold, proof*

fourteen strokes

擠[4] dzi *to squeeze*
擡[2] tai *to carry*
擬[4] i *to intend to*
擱[1] goh *to place*

fifteen strokes

擺[3] bai *to arrange*
擻[3] lou *upper story*
擾[3] rao *to trouble*
攀[1] pan *to scramble*
擦[1] tsah *to rub; wipe*
擄[1] lo *to capture*
擴[4] kwoh *to expand*

sixteen strokes

攏[3] lung *to embrace*

攘2 rang *to steal*
攙1 chan *to mix*
攔2 lan *to hinder*
eighteen strokes
攤1 tan *a stall*
twelve strokes
攪3 giao *to agitate*

65

支1 djĭh

66

攴 puh *to tap*
two strokes
收1 shou *to receive*
three strokes
改3 gai *to change*
攻1 gung *to attack*
four strokes
放4 fang *to loosen*
政4 djeng *government*
five strokes
故4 gu *a reason*
six strokes
效4 hsiao *to imitate*
seven strokes
敍4 hsü *to relate*
教1 giao *to teach*
敏3 min *clever*
救4 giu *to save*
敗4 bai *defeated*
eight strokes
敝4 bi *inferior*
敢3 gan *to dare*
散4 san *to scatter*
敦1 dun *honest*
nine strokes
敬4 ging *to reverence*
ten strokes
敲1 giao *to knock*
eleven strokes
敵2 dih *an enemy*
敷1 fu *diffuse*
數4 shu *a number*
twelve strokes
整3 djeng *to rectify*
斂3 lien *to collect*
fourteen strokes
斃4 bi *to die*

67

文2 wen *letters*
seven strokes
斌1 bin *elegant*
eight strokes
斑1 ban *a class*

68

斗3 dou *a bushel*
six strokes
料2 liao *materials*
seven strokes
斜2 hsie *deflected*
斟1 djeng *deliberate*

69

斤1 gin *an axe, a pound*
one stroke
斥4 chĭh *to destroy*
four strokes
斧3 fu *an axe*
seven strokes
斬3 djan *to decapitate*
eight strokes
斯1 szĭ *this*
nine strokes
新1 hsin *new*
fourteen strokes
斷4 dwan *to break off*

70

方1 fang *square*
four strokes
於2 yü *a particle*
five strokes
施1 shĭ *to bestow*
six strokes
旁2 pang *the side*
旅3 lü *a traveller*
seven strokes
旋2 hsüen *to revolve*
族2 dzuh *a tribe*
ten strokes
旗2 chi *a flag*

71

无 wu *not*
seven strokes
既4 gi *since*

72

日 rĭh *the sun*

one stroke

旦^{4} dan *sunrise*

two strokes

旨^{3} djĭ *will*

早^{3} dzao *early*

旬^{2} hsün *ten days*

旱^{4} han *drought*

four strokes

旺^{4} wang *to flourish*

昂^{2} ang *exalted*

昆^{1} kwen *elder brother*

昇^{1} sheng *to ascend*

昌^{1} chang *to flourish*

明^{2} ming *clear*

昏^{1} hwen *dull, clouded*

易^{4} ih *easy, to change*

昔^{2} hsih *formerly*

five strokes

星^{1} hsing *a star*

春^{1} chwen *spring*

昧^{4} mei *darkened*

昨^{2} dzoh *yesterday*

昭^{1} djao *bright*

是^{4} shĭ *verb to be*

six strokes

時^{2} shĭ *time*

晃^{3} huang *dazzling*

晏^{4} yen *a feast*

晌^{4} shang *noon*

seven strokes

晚^{3} wan *evening*

晝^{4} djou *day-time*

晦^{4} hwei *obscure*

晨^{2} chen *morning*

eight strokes

普^{3} pu *universal*

景^{3} ging *brilliant*

晴^{2} ching *clear*

晷^{1} gwei *a sun-dial*

智^{4} djĭ *wisdom*

nine strokes

暇^{4} hsia *leisure*

暈^{4} yün *giddy*

暑^{3} shu *the dog days*

暗^{4} an *dark*

ten strokes

暢^{4} chang *joy*

eleven strokes

暫^{4} dzan *temporary*

暮^{4} mo *evening*

暴^{4} bao *fierce*

twelve strokes

曆^{4} li *to pass over*

曉^{3} hsiao *enlighten*

fourteen strokes

曚^{2} meng *dark*

曜^{4} yao *glorious, a star*

fifteen strokes

曠^{4} kwang *wilderness*

nineteen strokes

曬^{4} shai *to sun*

73

曰 yüeh *to speak*

two strokes

曲^{1} chüh *crooked*

three strokes

更 geng *to change*

six strokes

書^{1} shu *a book*

eight strokes

曾^{2} tseng *previously*

替^{4} ti *to substitute*

最^{4} dzui *very*

會^{4} hwei *to congregate*

74

月 yüeh *the moon*

two strokes

有^{3} yu *to have*

four strokes

朋^{2} peng *a friend*

服^{2} fuh *to serve*

six strokes

朔^{4} soh *first day of moon*

朗^{4} lang *bright*

望4 wang *full moon*

eight strokes

朝 1 djao *morning*; 2 chao *the court*

期2 chi *a season*

75

木 muh *a tree*

one stroke

未4 wei *not yet*

本3 ben *a root, origin*

札1 djah *despatch*

末4 moh *end, last*

three strokes

朱1 dju *red*

朽3 hsiu *rotten*

three strokes

李3 li *plum tree*

杏1 hsing *apricot*

材2 tsai *timber*

村1 tswen *a village*

杖4 djang *a staff*

杜4 du *to stop up*

束4 shuh *to bind, tie*

four strokes

杪1 miao *tip, a moment*

杭2 hang *to sail, a boat*

杯1 bei *a cup*

東1 dung *east*

松1 sung *fir tree*

板3 ban *a board*

枉3 wang *bent, wrong*

枕3 djen *pillow*

林2 lin *a forest*

枚2 mei *one piece*

果3 go *certainly*

枝1 djï *a branch*

架4 gia *a frame*

柄4 bing *a handle*

柏3 beh *cedar*

某3 mou *a certain one*

柑1 gan *the orange*

染3 ran *to dye*

柔2 rou *pliant*

查2 cha *to search*

柩4 giu *a coffin*

柰4 nai *no alternative*

柱4 dju *a pillar*

柳3 liu *the willow*

柴2 chai *firewood*

柵2 djah *fence*

six strokes

栖1 hsi *to perch*

栗4 lih *chestnut*

校4 giao, *to compare*; hsiao, *a school*

根1 gen *a root*

格2 geh *a rule*

栽1 dzai *to plant*

桃2 tao *a peach*

案4 an *a table*

桑1 sang *the mulberry*

seven strokes

桶3 tung *a bucket*

梁2 liang *a beam*

梅2 mei *a plum*

梗3 geng *to obstruct*

條2 tiao *a wand, length*

梨2 li *pear tree*

梭1 so *a shuttle*

梯1 ti *a ladder*

械4 giai *weapons*

梳1 su, shu *to comb*

桿3 gan *club, staff*

eight strokes

犂2 li *a plough*

棄4 chi *to reject*

棉2 mien *cotton*

棒3 bang *a club*

棗3 dzao *a date tree*

棘4 gih *thorns*

棚2 peng *a stockade*

棟4 dung *a beam*

棠2 tang *the crab-apple*
棧4 djan *a warehouse*
森1 sen *gloomy*
棲1 hsi *to roost*
棹1 djoh *table*
棺1 gwan *a coffin*
椅3 i *a chair*
棍4 gwen *a club*

nine strokes

椶1 dzung *a palm*
楊2 yang *the willow*
楚3 tsu *plain, coarse*
楣2 mei *a lintel*
業4 yeh *an industry*
極2 gih *extreme*
楷3 chiai *pattern*

ten strokes

榜3 bang *notice board*
榖3 guh *grain*
榮2 yung *glory*
榻4 tah *bed, sofa*
槅3 geh *separate*
構4 gou *construct*
槍1 chiang *a spear*
槐2 hwai *the ash*

eleven strokes

槳3 dziang *an oar*
槽2 tsao *a trough*
樂4 loh *happiness*
樓2 lou *upper story*
標1 biao *standard*
樟1 djang *camphor tree*
模1 mo *a pattern*
樣4 yang *a kind*
概4 gai *generally*

twelve strokes

樸4 puh *honest*
樹4 shu *a tree*
橋2 chiao *a bridge*
凳4 deng *a stool*
機1 gi *piston, machine*
橡4 hsiang *oak*
橫2 hwen } *crosswise,*
hung } *perverse*

thirteen strokes

檀2 tan *sandalwood*
檢2 gien *restriction, model.*
櫃4 gwei *a cupboard*

fifteen strokes

櫛2 dzieh *a comb*
欄2 lan *a railing*
權2 chüen *power*
欖3 lan *olive tree*

76

欠 chien *to owe*

two strokes

次4 tsï *next in order*

four strokes

欣1 hsin *pleased*

six strokes

欲4 yüh *to desire*
欵3 kwan *expenditure, liberal*

eight strokes

欺1 chi *to cheat*
欽1 chin *imperial*
歇1 hsieh *to rest*

ten strokes

歉4 chieh } *be a-*
chien } *shamed*
歌1 go *a song*

eleven strokes

歎4 tan *to sigh*
歐1 ou *to vomit*

eighteen strokes

歡1 hwan *pleased*

77

止 djï *to stop*

one stroke

正4 djeng *upright*

two strokes

此3 tsï *this*

three strokes

步4 bu *a step*

four strokes

武3 wu *military*

twelve strokes

歷4 lih *to pass over*

fourteen strokes

歸 1 gwei *to return*

78

歹 dai *vicious*

two strokes

死 3 szï *to die*

four strokes

歿 4 muh *to be dead*

殀 3 yao *to die young*

five strokes

殃 1 yang *calamity*

殆 4 dai *very, exhausted*

six strokes

殉 4 hsün *desire, die for*

殊 2 shu *to kill, exceed*

eight strokes

殘 2 tsan *to injure*

殞 3 yün *to die*

thirteen strokes

殮 4 lien *to encoffin*

fourteen strokes

殯 4 bin *funeral*

79

殳 shu *a quarter-staff*

five strokes

段 4 dwan *a section*

six strokes

殷 1 yin *sincere*

seven strokes

殺 4 shah *to kill*

殼 4 koh *husk*

nine strokes

殿 4 dien *a temple*

毀 3 hui *break, destroy*

eleven strokes

毅 4 i *brave*

毆 3 ou *to beat*

80

毋 2 wu *a negative*

母 3 mu *mother*

three strokes

每 3 mei *each*

four strokes

毒 2 duh *poison*

81

比 bi *compare*

82

毛 2 mao *hair, fur*

five strokes

毡 1 djan *felt*

six strokes

毫 2 hao *tip of a hair*

eight strokes

毯 3 tan *a carpet*

thirteen strokes

氈 1 djan *felt*

83

氏 4 shï *a name*

民 2 min *people*

氓 2 meng *vagabonds*

84

气 chi *vapour*

氛 1 fen *vapour*

氣 4 chi *breath, temper*

85

水 shui *water*

氷 1 bing *ice*

永 3 yung *eternal*

two strokes

汁 1 djïh *juice*

求 2 chiu *to beseech*

three strokes

汎 4 fan *an expanse*

汙 1 wu *dirty*

汗 4 han *drought*

汛 4 hsün *to patrol*

汝 3 rü *pronoun, you*

汞 3 hung *cinnabar*

江 1 giang *a river*

池 2 chï *a pool*

four strokes

汪 1 wang *the ocean*

汰 4 tai *to eliminate*

汲 1 gih *draw water*

汴 4 bien *name of river*

決 2 güeh *decide, certainly*

汾 1 fen *a river*

沈 2 chen *to sink*
沐 4 muh *to bathe*
沒 4 muh *disappear, not*
沖 1 chung *dash against*
沙 1 sha *sand*
沛 4 pei *soaking*

five strokes

沫 4 moh *froth*
河 2 ho *a river*
沸 4 fuh *boiling*
油 2 yu *oil*
治 4 djï *to govern*
沽 1 gu *to buy*
沾 1 djan *to encroach*
沿 2 yen *follow course of R.*
況 4 kwang *moreover*
泄 4 i *to leak*
泉 2 tsüen *a fountain*
泊 2 beh *to anchor*
法 1 fah *a law*
泗 4 szï *a river*
泛 4 fan *a flood*
泡 4 pao *a bubble*
波 1 bo *a wave*
泣 4 chih *to sob*
泥 2 ni *mud*
注 4 dju *attention*
泮 4 pan *pool*
泯 3 min *a river*
泰 4 tai *exalt d*

six strokes

洋 2 yang *ocean, foreign*
洒 3 sa *scatter water*
洗 3 hsi *to wash*
洛 4 loh *a river*
洞 4 dung *a cave*
津 1 dzin *a ford*
洩 4 hsieh *to leak*
洪 2 hung *vast*
洲 1 djou *an island, continent*
活 2 hoh *living*
洽 4 hsiah *mix, harmoniz*
派 4 pai *tribe, to send*

seven strokes

流 2 liu *to flow*
浙 4 djeh *a river*
浡 4 poh *full, bursting*
浦 3 pu *a creek*
浩 4 hao *vast*
浪 4 lang *a wave*
浮 2 fou *float*
浴 4 yuh *bathe*
海 3 hai *sea*
浸 4 dzin *soak, immerse*
涇 1 ging *a river*
消 1 hsiao *melt*
涉 4 sheh *ford, involve*
涎 2 yen *saliva*
涕 4 ti *to weep*

eight strokes

涯 2 yai *a bank*
液 4 ih *secretions*
涵 2 han *to contain*
涸 4 heh *to dry up*
涼 2 liang *cool*
淅 4 djeh *a river*
淆 2 yao *muddy, mixed*
淋 2 lin *to drip*
淑 4 shuh *pure*
淒 1 tsi *freezing, cruel*
淘 2 tao *wash, eliminate*
淚 4 lei *tears*
淡 4 dan *insipid*
淤 1 yü *silt*
淨 4 dzing *pure*
淪 2 lwen *lost*
淮 2 hwai *river*
淫 2 yin *fornication*

深 1 shen *deep*
淵 1 yüen *deep pool*
混 4 hwen *muddy, chaotic*
清 1 tsing *clear*
淹 1 yen *drowned*
淺 3 chien *shallow*
添 1 tien *to add to*

nine strokes

減 3 gien *reduce*
渠 2 chü *a ditch*
渡 4 du *to ferry*
溫 1 wen *warm*
測 4 tseh *to measure*
渭 4 wei *a river*
港 3 giang *a harbour*
渴 3 koh *thirsty*
游 2 yu *to ramble*
渺 3 miao *vast, vague*
渾 2 hwen *confused, the whole*
湃 4 bai *to splash*
湊 4 tsou *collect*
湖 2 hu *a lake*
湘 1 hsiang *a river*
湛 4 djan *clear*
湼 1 nieh *traduce, defile*
湧 3 yung *spout forth*
湯 1 tang *soup*

ten strokes

滙 4 hwei *waters meeting*
源 2 yüen *a fountain, origin*
準 3 djwen *to grant*
溝 1 gou *a drain*
溜 4 liu *slippery*
溢 4 ih *to overflow*
溪 1 hsi *a stream*
溯 4 su *ascend the stream*
溺 4 nih *to drown*
溼 1 shïh *wet*
滅 4 mieh *destroy*
滇 1 dien *a river*
滋 1 dzï *to soak*
滌 2 dih *to wash*
滑 2 hwah *slippery*
滓 2 dzï *dregs*
滕 2 deng *bubbling up*

eleven strokes

滴 1 dih *a drop*
滸 3 hu *a lake*
滿 3 man *full*
漁 2 yü *to fish*
漂 1 piao *to float*
漆 1 chih *varnish*
漏 4 lou *to strain*
演 3 yen *to arrange*
漕 2 tsao *tribute*
漠 4 moh *a desert*
漢 4 han *a river*
漩 2 hsüen *a whirlpool*
漫 4 man *extensive*
漬 4 dzï *soaked*
漲 4 djang *increase*
漸 1 dzien *gradually*
漿 1 dziang *soy*

twelve strokes

潑 1 poh *empty out*
潔 2 gieh *pure*
潤 4 rwen *to moisten*
潦 3 lao *a flood*
潭 2 tan *a pool*
潮 2 chao *flood tide*
潰 4 kwei *debacle*
澄 2 deng *to cleanse*
澆 1 giao *to sprinkle*
澈 4 cheh *limpid*

twelve strokes

澡 3 dzao *bathe*
澤 2 dzeh *a marsh*
激 1 gih *impetuous*
濁 2 djoh *filthy*

濃 2 nung *thick*

fourteen strokes

濕 1 shĭh *wet*

濟 4 tsi *ferry, help*

濤 2 tao *billows*

濫 4 lan *excessive*

濯 2 djoh *purify*

濱 1 bin *coast*

fifteen strokes

濺 4 gien *splashed*

瀆 5 duh *to defile*

瀑 4 bao *a waterfall*

sixteen strokes

灌 4 gwan *to water*

灘 1 tan *shoal*

86

火 ho *fire*

two strokes

灰 1 hwei *ashes*

three strokes

灼 2 shoh *burn, clean*

災 1 dzai *calamity*

four strokes

炊 1 chui *to boil*

炎 2 yen *hot*

炒 3 chao *to roast*

炕 4 kang *a brick bed*

炙 4 djĭh *to broil*

five strokes

炭 4 tan *charcoal*

炮 2 pao *to roast*

six strokes

烈 4 lieh *white heat*

烏 1 wu *black*

烘 1 hung *to warm*

烙 4 loh *to brand*

烤 3 kao *bake, roast*

seven strokes

烹 1 peng *to cook*

烽 1 feng *a beacon*

焉 1 yen *a particle interrogative*

eight strokes

焙 4 bei *to heat*

焚 2 fen *to burn up*

無 2 wu *without*

焦 1 giao *scorched, vexed*

然 2 ran *but, nevertheless*

nine strokes

煅 4 dwan *to refine*

煇 1 hwei *brilliant*

煌 2 hwang *bright*

煎 1 dzien *to fry*

煑 3 dju *to boil*

煕 1 hsi *flourishing*

煖 3 nwan *warm*

煙 1 yen *smoke*

煞 4 shah *very*

焰 4 yen *flame, glare*

煤 2 mei *coal*

煥 4 hwan *flaming*

照 4 djao *bright, clear*

煨 1 wei *cook, boil*

煩 2 fan *to trouble*

煽 1 shan *to flame, excite*

熄 1 hsih *extinguish*

熊 2 hsiung *a bear*

熏 1 hsün *incense, merit*

熟 2 shuh *cooked, ripe*

熬 2 ao *to simmer*

熱 4 reh *hot*

twelve strokes

熾 4 chĭh *a blaze*

燈 1 deng *a lamp*

燉 4 dwen *to stew*

燎 4 liao *beacon*

燒 1 shao *to burn*

燕 4 yen *the swallow*

燃 2 ran *to scorch*

thirteen strokes

營 2 ying *camp, to plan*

燥 4 dzao *very hot*

燦 4 tsan *shining*

燭 2 djuh *a candle*

燻1 hsün *to fumigate*
燼4 dzin *ashes*
爆4 bao *fire-crackers*
爐2 lu *stove*

seventeen strokes

爛4 lan *over-cooked*

twenty-five strokes

爨4 tsuan *a furnace*

87

爪3 djao *talons*

four strokes

爬2 pa *to creep*
爭1 dzeng *to strive*

five strokes

爲2 wei *to be, to do*

fourteen strokes

爵2 dzioh *nobility*

88

父4 fu *father*
爸1 ba *papa*

six strokes

爹1 die *father*

nine strokes

爺2 ye *grandfather, an official*

89

爻 yao *crosswise*
爽3 shwang *lively*
爾3 er *pronoun, you*

90

爿 chiang *reversed*
牀2 chwang *a bed*
牆2 chiang *a wall*

91

片4 pien *a splinter*
版3 ban *a board*
牌2 pai *a signboard*
牒2 dieh *a despatch*
牕1 chwang *a window*
牘2 duh *a letter*

92

牙2 ya *a molar*

93

牛2 niu *an ox*

two strokes

牝3 pin *female*

three strokes

牡3 mou *male*
牢2 lao *a prison*

four strokes

牧4 muh *a shepherd*
物4 wuh *a thing*

five strokes

牯3 gu *a bull*
牲1 seng *animals*
牴3 di *to butt*

six strokes

特4 teh *specially*

seven strokes

牽1 chien *to lead*
犀1 hsi *rhinoceros*
犁2 li *to plough*

ten strokes

犒4 kao *a reward*

fifteen strokes

犢2 duh *a calf*

sixteen strokes

犧1 hsi *to sacrifice*

94

犬 chüen *a dog*

two strokes

犯4 fan *to transgress*

four strokes

狀4 djwang *appearance*
狂2 kwang *madness*
狄2 dih *savage tribe*

five strokes

狎2 hsiah *dalliance*
狐2 hu *a fox*
狗3 gou *a dog*
狩4 shou *to hunt*

seven strokes

狸2 li *a fox*
狼2 lang *a wolf*
狽4 bei *demoralized*

eight strokes

猖1 chang *vicious*

猛³ meng *fierce*
猜¹ tsai *to guess*
nine strokes
猩¹ hsing *a monkey*
猪¹ dju *a pig*
猫² mao *a cat*
猴² hou *monkey*
猶² yu *to hesitate*
ten strokes
猾² hwah *tricky*
獃¹ dai *silly*
猿² yüen *a baboon*
獄⁴ yüh *a prison, hell*
獅¹ szï *a lion*
eleven strokes
獐¹ djang *a deer*
twelve strokes
獨² duh *alone*
fourteen strokes
獲⁴ hwoh *to capture*
fifteen strokes
獵⁴ lieh *to hunt*
獸⁴ shou *animal*
sixteen strokes
獺³ tah *an otter*
獻⁴ hsien *to offer*

95

玄² hsüen *black*
率⁴ shwai, *to lead* lüh, *a limit*

96

玉 yüh *a gem*
王² wang *king*
three strokes
玩⁴ wan *a plaything*
five strokes
玲² ling *tinkling*
玳⁴ dai *a gem*
玷⁴ dien *a blemish*
玼² tzï *a flaw*
珀⁴ peh *amber*
珊¹ shan *coral*
珍¹ djen *pearls*
玻¹ bo *glass*
six strokes
珠¹ dju *a pearl*
珪¹ gwei *a sceptre*
班¹ ban *a class*
珮⁴ pei *to wear*
seven strokes
現⁴ hsien *to manifest*
球² chiu *a ball*
理³ li *reason*
eight strokes
琢² djoh *to cut gems*
琥³ hu *amber*
琴² chin *a harp*
琶¹ ba *a guitar*
nine strokes
瑙³ nao *agate*
瑕² hsia *a flaw*
瑚² hu *coral*
瑞⁴ shui *auspicious*
瑟⁴ seh *a flute*
ten strokes
瑣³ so *fragments*
瑰⁴ gwei *jasper*
eleven strokes
璃² li *glass*
thirteen strokes
璧⁴ bih *a seal*
環² hwan *a ring*
fourteen strokes
璽³ hsi *the Imperial seal*

97

瓜¹ gwa *a melon*
eleven strokes
瓢² piao *a gourd*
fourteen strokes
瓣⁴ ban *section of an orange*
seventeen strokes
瓤² rang *pith, core*

98

瓦³ wa *a tile*
seven strokes
瓶² ping *a bottle*
nine strokes
甄¹ djen *to separate*

甎 1 djwan *a brick*

thirteen strokes

甕 4 wong *a jar*

99

甘 1 gan *sweet*

four strokes

甚 4 shen *very*

six strokes

甜 2 tien *sweet*

100

生 1 seng *life*

six strokes

產 3 chan *give birth to*

seven strokes

甥 1 seng *maternal nephew*

甦 1 su *rejuvenate*

101

用 4 yung *use*

two strokes

甫 3 fu *begin*

102

田 2 tien *a field*

由 2 yu *from*

甲 3 giah *the first*

申 1 shen *to explain*

two strokes

男 2 nan *male*

four strokes

界 4 giai *frontier*

畏 4 wei *to fear*

five strokes

畔 4 ban *a boundary*

留 2 liu *to detain*

畜 4 chuh *animals*

畝 3 mou *an acre*

six strokes

畢 2 bih *finished*

略 2 lioh *somewhat*

seven strokes

番 1 fan *barbarian*

畫 4 hwa *paint, draw*

異 4 i *strange, different*

當 1 dang *ought, to pawn*

fourteen strokes

疆 1 giang *a boundary*

sixteen strokes

疊 2 dieh *piled up*

103

疋 pih *a roll of cloth*

seven strokes

疏 1 su *wide, distant*

nine strokes

疑 2 i *to doubt*

104

疒 nih *a disease*

three strokes

疝 4 shan *hernia*

疥 1 giai *itch*

疫 4 ih *pestilence*

five strokes

疲 2 pi *wearied*

疵 2 tzï *fault, flaw*

疹 3 djen *spots, rash*

疽 1 dzü *ulcer*

疾 2 dzih *sickness*

病 4 bing *disease*

症 4 djeng *disease*

six strokes

痊 2 tsüen *cured*

痔 4 chï *hemorrhoids*

疼 2 teng *pain, love*

痗 4 mei *bad luck*

痕 2 hen *a scar*

痛 4 tung *painful*

痞 3 pi *constipation*

痢 4 li *dysentery*

eight strokes

痰 2 tan *mucous*

nine strokes

瘉 4 yü *convalescent*

瘋 1 feng *mad*

ten strokes

瘠 2 dzih *lean, thin*

瘢 1 ban *an eruption*

瘤 2 liu *a wen*

瘧 4 nioh *fever*

瘦[4] sou *lean, thin*
瘟[1] wen *pestilence*
瘡[1] chuang *sore*

eleven strokes

癩[4] lai *scab, leprosy*
癬[3] hsien *ringworm*
癰[1] yung *an ulcer*

105

癶 boh *back to back*
癸[3] gwei *the tenth stem*

seven strokes

登[1] deng *to ascend*
發[1] fah *issue forth*

106

白[2] beh *white*
百[3] beh *one hundred*

two strokes

皁[4] dzao *black*

three strokes

的[1] dih *possessive particle*

four strokes

皆[1] giai *all*
皇[2] hwang *an Emperor*

five strokes

皎[3] giao *bright*

107

皮[2] pi *skin*

five strokes

皺[4] dzou *wrinkles*

108

皿[3] hsüeh *blood*

three strokes

盂[2] yü *a dish*

four strokes

盅[1] djung *a cup*
盆[2] pen *a basin, tub*
盈[2] ying *overflowing*

five strokes

益[2] ih *advantage*
盌[3] wan *a basin*
盍[2] hoh *why not?*
盔[1] kuei *helmet*

seven strokes

盛 2cheng { *to fill*; 4sheng { *abundant*
盜[4] dao *to steal*

eight strokes

盟[2] meng *a covenant*
盞[3] djan *a saucer*
蓋[4] gai *a cover*

nine strokes

盡[4] dzin *fulfil, exhaust*
監[1] gien *to oversee*

ten strokes

盤[2] pan *a plate, to examine*

109

目[4] muh *the eye*

three strokes

盲[2] mang *blind*
直[2] djïh *straight*

four strokes

相[1] hsiang *mutual*
盼[4] pan *to expect*
盾[4] dun *a shield*
省 3sheng { *a province*; hsing { *to examine*
眇[3] miao *minute, subtle*
眉[2] mei *eyebrows*
看[1] kan *to look*
眞[1] djen *real, actual*
眠[2] mien *to sleep*

six strokes

眶[2] kwang *eye sockets*
眷[4] güen *to love*
眼[3] yen *eyes*
衆[4] djung *many, all*

eight strokes

睛[1] dzing *the iris*
睡[4] shui *to sleep*
督[1] duh *to oversee*
睦[4] muh *peaceful*
睫[4] dzieh *eyelashes*

ten strokes

瞋[1] chen *angry*
瞎[1] hsiah *blind*

eleven strokes

瞞[2] man *to deceive*

twelve strokes

瞬^{4} shun *to wink*

瞳^{2} tung *the pupil*

thirteen strokes

瞽^{4} gu *blind*

瞿^{4} gü *to fear*

fourteen strokes

矇^{2} meng *dark*

110

矛^{2} mou *a spear*

111

矢^{3} shïh *a dart*

矣^{3} i *final particle*

three strokes

知^{1} djï *to know*

five strokes

矩^{3} gü *a square, proper*

seven strokes

短^{3} dwan *short*

eight strokes

矮^{3} ai *low of stature*

thirteen strokes

矯^{3} giao *to dissemble*

112

石^{2} shïh *a stone*

four strokes

砂^{1} sha *sand*

砌^{4} tsi *to build*

five strokes

砭^{1} bien *probe, blame*

砰^{1} peng *dash against*

砲^{4} pao *ballista*

破^{4} po *to break*

six strokes

研^{2} yen *to examine*

seven strokes

硝^{1} hsiao *nitre*

硬^{4} ying *hard*

硯^{4} yen *an ink-slab*

eight strokes

碗^{3} wan *bowl*

碰^{4} peng *to run against*

碎^{4} sui *fragments*

碑^{1} bei *memorial stone*

碓^{4} dui *pestle*

nine strokes

碧^{4} bih *jade*

碩^{4} shoh *large*

碪^{1} djen *an anvil*

ten strokes

碾^{3} nien *a roller*

磁^{2} tzï *pottery*

磅^{1} pang *a pound*

磋^{1} tso *to grind*

磐^{1} pan *a rock*

磕^{1} koh *to knock, kotow*

eleven strokes

磚^{1} djwan *a brick*

磨^{2} mo *a mill-stone*

磬^{4} ching *to tinkle*

twelve strokes

磯^{1} gi *a ledge*

磴^{4} deng *a step*

磽^{1} chiao *barren land*

thirteen strokes

礎^{3} tsu *a foundation*

fourteen strokes

礙^{4} ai *a hindrance*

礦^{3} gung *a mine*

礪^{4} li *rubble*

礫^{4} lih *gravel*

礬^{1} fan *alum*

sixteen strokes

礮^{4} pao *ballista*

113

示^{4} shï *an omen*

three strokes

社^{4} she *society*

祀^{4} szï *sacrifice*

祈^{2} chi *to pray*

祉^{3} djï *good fortune*

five strokes

祐^{4} yu *favour*

祖^{3} dzu *ancestors*

祚^{4} dzu *honours*

祜^{4} hu *blessing*

祝^{4} djuh *to bless*

神2 shen *gods, spirits*
祟4 sui *malign influence*
祠2 tzï *ancestral worship*
six strokes
祥2 hsiang *fortunate*
票4 piao *certificate, ticket*
祭4 dzi *to sacrifice*
eight strokes
祿4 luh *emoluments*
禀3 bing *permission, petition*
禁4 gin *to forbid*
nine strokes
禍4 ho *calamity*
禎1 djen *fortunate*
福2 fuh *happiness*
ten strokes
禦4 yü *to oppose*
禧1 hsi *good fortune*
禪2 chan *meditation*
thirteen strokes
禮3 li *propriety*
fourteen strokes
禱3 dao *prayer*

114

禸 rou *footprint*
禹3 yü *ancient Emperor*
禽2 chin *birds*

115

禾 ho *grain*
two strokes
秀4 hsiu *flourishing*
私1 szï *selfish*
three strokes
秉3 bing *a handful, rule*
four strokes
秋1 chiu *autumn*
科1 ko *series, science*
秒3 miao *the tip, a moment*
five strokes
租1 dzu *rent*
秤4 cheng *to weigh*
秦2 tsin *ancient State*
秧1 yang *sprouting rice*
秩4 djïh *rank, series*
秘4 bi *secret*
six strokes
移2 i *to remove*
seven strokes
稀1 hsi *seldom, thin*
稅4 shui *taxes*
稉1 geng *kind of rice*
程2 cheng *a stage*
稍1 shao *slightly*
稗4 bai *weeds*
稚4 djï *young*
稟3 lin *granary*
稠2 chou *dense*
nine strokes
稭3 giai *grain stalks*
種3 djung *seed, a class*
稱1 cheng *to style*
ten strokes
稿3 gao *rough copy*
稻4 dao *rice grain*
稼4 gia *harvest*
穀3 guh *grain*
eleven strokes
穅1 kang *chaff*
穆4 moh *reverential*
稺4 djï *young*
穌1 su *to revive*
積1 dzih *to accumulate*
穎3 ying *clever*
穗4 sui *ears of grain*
穡5 seh *harvest*
穢4 huei *dirty*
fourteen strokes
穩3 wen *firm*
穫1 hwoh *to reap*

116

穴4 hsüeh *a cave*
two strokes
究4 giu *investigate*
three strokes
穹2 chiung *empyrean*

空1 kung *empty*

four strokes

穿1 chwan *put on clothes*

突4 tuh *suddenly*

five strokes

窄4 dzeh *narrow*

窈3 yao *a deep cave*

six strokes

窒4 djih *to impede*

seven strokes

窗1 chwang *a window*

窘3 giung *afflicted*

eight strokes

窟1 kuh *a hole*

窠1 ko *a nest*

nine strokes

窩1 wo *a nest*

窪1 wa *a depression*

窮2 chiung *poor*

eleven strokes

窺1 kwei *to spy*

窻1 chwang *window*

窿2 lung *a hole*

thirteen strokes

竄4 tswan *to sneak away*

竅4 chiao *an orifice*

fifteen strokes

竇4 dou *a name*

sixteen strokes

竈4 dzao *kitchen range*

竊4 tsieh *to steal*

117

立4 lih *to set up*

five strokes

站4 djan *to stand*

six strokes

竟4 ging *then, at last*

章1 djang *a chapter*

seven strokes

竣1 gün *finished*

童2 tung *a youth*

竦3 sung *to rise up*

eight strokes

竪4 shu *to set up*

nine strokes

竭2 gieh *extremely*

端1 dwan *correct*

fourteen strokes

競4 ging *to strive*

118

竹 djuh *bamboo*

two strokes

竺2 djuh *India*

three strokes

竿1 gan *a stick*

four strokes

笆1 ba *a fence*

笋3 swen *bamboo shoots*

笑4 hsiao *to laugh*

five strokes

笙1 seng *a lute*

笛2 dih *a flute*

笞1 chï *a club, to beat*

符2 fu *a charm*

第4 di *ordinal number*

笨4 ben *stupid*

six strokes

筆3 bih *a Chinese pen*

等3 deng *an order, series*

筋1 gin *sinews*

筏2 fah *a raft*

筐1 kwang *a basket*

筒2 tung *a tube*

答2 dah *to reply*

策4 chieh *a plan*

seven strokes

筵2 yen *a feast*

eight strokes

箇4 go *classifier, one*

箋1 gien *note paper*

箏1 dzeng *a kite*

箒3 djou *a switch, broom*

箕1 gi *a sieve, basket*

算4 swan *to reckon*

箝2 chien *tweezers*

管3 gwan *to govern*

nine strokes

箭4 dzien *an arrow*

箱1 hsiang *a box*

箴[1] djen *to probe*
箸[4] dju *chop-sticks*
節[3] dzieh *bamboo joint, regulation*
範[4] fan *a model*
篆[4] djwan *seal character*
篇[1] pien *a section*
築[2] djuh *to raise*

ten strokes

篙[1] gao *a pole*
篤[3] duh *firmly*
篦[1] bi *a small comb*
篩[1] shai *a sieve*

eleven strokes

篷[2] peng *a sail*
篾[4] mieh *bamboo splints*
簡[3] gien *to abridge*
簧[2] hwang *reed, spring*
簫[1] hsiao *flageolet, lonely*

twelve strokes

簽 chien *a slip, to endorse*
簷[2] yen *eaves*
簸[3] bo *dust-pan*
簾[2] lien *a screen*
簿[4] pu *an account book*

fourteen strokes

籃[2] lan *a basket*
籌[2] chon *calculate, discuss*
籍[2] dzih *books, census*

sixteen strokes

籠[2] lung *a muzzle*

seventeen strokes

籤[1] chien *slip, a lot*
籥[4] yoh *a flute*

nineteen strokes

籬[2] li *a fence*
籮[2] lo *large basket*

119

米[3] mi *rice*
粧[1] djuang *to decorate*

four strokes

粉[3] fen *flour, powder*

five strokes

粒[4] lih *a grain*
粘[2] nien *sticky*
粗[1] tsu *coarse*

six strokes

粟[4] su *maize*
粵[4] yüeh *Canton province*
粥[1] djuh *congee*

seven strokes

粱[2] liang *millet*

eight strokes

粹[4] sui *pure*
精[1] dzing *kernel, semen*

nine strokes

糊[2] hu *paste, confused*

ten strokes

糕[1] gao *rice cakes*
糖[2] tang *rice dumplings*

eleven strokes

糞[4] fen *manure*
糟[1] dzao *rotten, dregs*
糠[1] kang *husk, chaff*

twelve strokes

糧[2] liang *grain, food*

sixteen strokes

糴[2] dih *purchase grain*

nineteen strokes

糶[4] tiao *sell grain*

120

糸 szï *silk*

two strokes

糾[1] giu *entangled*

three strokes

紀[4] gi *to record*
約[4] yoh *a covenant*
紅[2] hung *red*

four strokes

紊[4] wen *confused*
紋[2] wen *refined*
納[4] nah *to give, to receive*
純[2] shwen *pure, sincere*
紗[1] sha *thread, crepe*
紙[3] djï *paper*
級[2] gih *an order, merit*
紛[1] fen *confused*

素[4] su *white, plain*
紡[3] fang *to spin*
索[4] soh *a rope*

five strokes

紫[3] tzï *purple*
紬[2] chou *woven silk*
累[4] lei *involved*
細[4] hsi *fine, minute*
紳[1] shen *gentry*
終[1] djung *end, finish*
組[3] dzu *weave, construct*
絆[4] ban *bind, trip*

six strokes

結[1] gieh *a knot*
絕[2] dzüeh *break, very*
絞[3] giao *twist, strangle*
絡[4] loh *to connect*
給[3] gih *to give*
絨[2] rung *velvet, flannel*
絮[4] hsü *gossamer, repetition*
統[3] tung *main rope, all*
絲[1] szï *silk thread*
絳[4] giang *crimson*

seven strokes

絹[4] güen *thin silk*
綠[4] luh *green*
綏[1] sui *quiet*
經[1] ging *warp, rule*
綁[3] bang *to bind*

eight strokes

綜[3] dzung *gather together*
綠[4] luh *green*
綢[2] chou *silk*
綫[4] hsien *thread*
維[2] wei *only, but*
綱[1] gang *main rope, bond, law*
網[3] wang *a net*
綵[3] tsai *gaudy*
綸[2] lwen *wind silk*
綻[4] djan *a rent*
綽[1] choh *spacious*
綾[2] ling *silk gauze*
綿[2] mien *cotton*
緒[4] hsü *a clue*
緘[2] hsien *seal, silent*
線[4] hsien *thread*
締[4] di *to bind*
緦[1] hsi *linen*
編[1] bien *weave, compose*
緩[3] hwan *slow*
緬[3] mien *silk thread, Burmah*
緯[4] wei *woof*
練[4] 2 lien *drill, practice*
緻[4] djï *fine, delicate*
緣[2] yüen *cause, affinity*

ten strokes

縊[4] ih *to hang*
縋[4] djui *suspend*
縐[4] dzou *crape*
縛[2] fuh *to bind*
縣[4] hsien *a district*

eleven strokes

縫[2] feng *to sew*
縮[1] soh *reduce*
縱[1] dzung *although, let go*
縶[4] djï *to tie up*
總[3] dzung *all, main*
績[1] dzih *merit*
繁[2] fan *multitudinous*

twelve strokes

織[1] djïh *to weave*
繕[4] shan *prepare, copy*
繙[1] fan *to translate*
繞[3] rao *wind, bind*
繡[4] hsiu *embroider*

thirteen strokes

繩[2] sheng *a rope*
繫[4] hsi *to gird up*
繭[3] gien *cocoons*

fourteen strokes

辮 4 bien *to plait, a queue*
繼 4 gi *to connect*
纂 4 dzwan *to usurp*

fifteen strokes

續 4 hsüh *to connect*
纍 2 lei *to bind*
纏 2 chan *to entangle*

seventeen strokes

纓 1 ying *tassels*
纔 2 tsai *thereupon, then*

nineteen strokes

纛 1 duh *a flag*

twenty-two strokes

纜 4 lan *a hawser*

121

缶 fou *pottery*

three strokes

缸 1 gang *a water-butt*

four strokes

缺 1 chüeh *be deficient*

six strokes

缾 ping *a bottle*

eleven strokes

罄 4 ching *empty*

twelve strokes

罇 1 tseng *a jar*

122

网 wang *a net*
罕 3 han *scarce, seldom*

three strokes

罔 3 wang *to deceive*
罩 4 djao *covering, shade*
罪 4 dzui *sin, crime*
置 4 djïh *to place*

nine strokes

罰 2 fah *to punish*
署 4 shu *official residence*

ten strokes

罵 4 ma *to revile*
罷 4 ba *ended, imperative*

eleven strokes

罹 2 li *incur*

fourteen strokes

羅 2 lo *net, gauze*
羈 1 gi *to tether*

123

羊 2 yang *a sheep*

three strokes

美 3 mei *pretty*
羔 1 gao *a lamb*

five strokes

羞 1 hsiu *ashamed*

seven strokes

羣 2 chün *a flock, many*
羨 4 hsien *to long for*
義 4 i *righteous*

thirteen strokes

羶 1 shan *rank, smell*

124

羽 yü *feathers*
翁 1 weng *old man, father*
翅 4 chï *wings*
翌 4 ih *to-morrow*
翎 2 ling *plumes*
習 2 hsih *to learn, skilled*
翔 2 hsiang *to hover*
翠 4 tsui *kingfisher, chrysoprase*
翡 3 fei *chrysoprase*
翰 4 han *to soar, letters*
翹 1 chiao *elevate, stilts*
翻 1 fang *to turn over*
翼 4 i *a wing, to assist*
耀 4 yao *illumine, glory*

125

老 3 lao *old*
考 3 kao *examine*
者 3 dje *which, this*
耆 2 chi *a man of sixty*

126

而 2 er *but, still, and*
耍 3 shua *sport, game*
耐 4 nai *sufferance*

127

耒[3] lei *a plough*
耕[1] geng *to plow*
耗[4] hao *diminish, waste*
耘[2] yün *to weed*
耙[2] pa *harrow*
耡[2] tsu *hoe, mattock*

128

耳[3] er *the ear*
耶[2] ye *father, how!*
耿[3] geng *bright, firm*
聆[2] ling *to hear*
聊[2] liao *to depend on*
聖[4] sheng *perfect, saint*
聘[4] ping *to engage, to betroth*
聚[4] dzü *to concentrate*
聞[2] wen *to hear, smell*
聯[2] lien *to connect, alliance*
聰[1] tsung *wise, acute*
聲[1] sheng *noise, sound*
聶[4] nieh *whisper*
職[2] djïh *duty, office*
聽[1] ting *to hear, obey*
聾[2] lung *deaf*

129

聿 yüh *Chinese pen*
肄[4] i *to learn, practise*
肅[4] suh *respectful, serious*
肆[4] szï *recklessly, four*
肇[4] djao *initiate, begin*

130

月[4] ruh *flesh*

two strokes

肋[4] leh *ribs*
肌[1] gi *flesh*
肖[4] hsiao *to resemble*
肘[3] djou *elbow*
肚[4] du *belly*
肛[1] gang *anus*
肝[1] gan *liver*

four strokes

股[3] gu *thighs, shares*
肢[1] dji *limbs*
肥[2] fei *stout, fat*
肩[1] gien *shoulder*
肫[1] djwen *gizzard*
肯[3] ken *be willing*
育[4] yüh *to bear, raise*
肴[2] hsiao *viands*
肺[4] fei *lung*

five strokes

胥[1] hsü *all, related*
胃[4] wei *stomach*
胆[3] dan *gall*
背[4] bei *back, depart*
胎[1] tai *womb*
胖[4] pan *stout, fat*
胞[1] bao *placenta, cell*
胡[2] hu *how, confusedly*
胭[1] yen *rouge*

six strokes

胰[2] i *soap*
胸[1] hsiung *thorax*
能[2] neng *ability, skill*
脂[1] dji *grease, fat*
脅[2] hsieh *ribs*
脈[4] meh *veins, pulse*
脊[2] dzih *spine*

seven strokes

脚[3] gioh *foot, foundation*
脣[2] chwen *lips*
脩[1] hsiu *tuition, long*
脫[1] toh *take off, cast away*
脬[1] pao *bladder*
脯[3] fu *dried meat*

eight strokes

脹[4] djang *swell*
脾[2] pi *spleen*

臘[1] lah *dried meat*
腎[4] shen *kidney*
腐[3] fu *rotten, old*
腑[1] fu *viscera*
腔[1] chiang *breast, tune*
腕[3] wan *wrist*

nine strokes

腥[1] hsing *rank, noisome*
腦[3] nao *brain*
腫[3] djung *bloated*
腰[1] yao *waist*
腳[3] gioh *foot, foundation*
腸[2] chang *bowels, intestines*
腮[1] sai *cheek*
腹[3] fuh *belly*

ten strokes

腿[3] tui *leg, ham*
膀[23] pang *bladder, arm*
膏[1] gao *grease, fat*
膚[3] fu *skin*
膛[2] tang *bosom, palate*
膜[4] moh *membrane, film*
膝[2] hsih *knee*
膠[1] giao *glue, gum*

twelve strokes

膨[2] peng *bloated, stout*
膩[4] ni *greasy, dirty*
膳[4] shan *food*
膽[3] dan *gall*
膿[2] nung *purulence, pus*
臂[4] bei *arm*

thirteen strokes

臉[3] lien *face*
臊[1] sao *rancid*
臍[2] tsi *navel*
臘[4] lah *cured meat*
臙[1] yen *rouge*
臟[4] dzang *viscera*

131

臣 chen *a statesman*
臥[4] wo *lie down, rest*
臧[1] tsang *store up*
臨[2] lin *attend, visit*

132

自[4] dzï *self, from*
臬[4] nieh *door post, statute*
臭[4] chou *stench*
臯[1] gao *high, eminent*

133

至[4] dji *to reach, most*
致[4] dji *cause, render*
臺[2] tai *terrace*
臻[1] djen *to reach*

134

臼[4] giu *a mortar*
臾[2] yü *a little while*
舀[3] yao *lade out*
舂[1] chung *pestle*
舅[4] giu *uncles, brothers-in-law*
與[3] yü *or, and*
興[1] hsing *arise, prosper*
舉[3] gü *uphold, raise*
舊[4] giu *old, ancient*

135

舌[2] sheh *tongue*
舍[4] she *lodge, cottage*
舒[1] shu *cheerful, open out*
舔[3] tien *lick*
舖[4] pu *shop*

136

舛 chwan *perverse*
舜[4] shwen *a name*
舞[3] wu *flourish, dance*

137

舟[1] djou *a boat*
舢[1] san *sampan*
航[2] hang *sail*

般[1] ban *kind, sort*
舵[4] do *rudder*
船[2] chwan *ship, boat*
艄[1] shao *stern*
艙[1] tsang *cabin, hold*

138

艮[4] geng *perverse*
良[2] liang *good, loyal*
艱[1] gien *difficult*

139

色[4] seh *colour, desire*
艷[4] yen *handsome, desire*

140

艸 tsao *grass*

two strokes

艾[4] ai *mugwort*
芋[4] yü *taro*
芙[2] fu *hibiscus*

four strokes

芝[1] djï *sesamum*
芟[2] shan *to mow*
芥[4] giai *mustard*
芬[1] fen *fragrant*
芭[1] ba *palm, plantain*
花[1] hua *flower*
芳[1] fang *fragrant*
芹[2] chin *celery*

five strokes

芻[2] chu *hay*
芽[2] ya *sprout*
苑[4] yüen *garden, park*
苔[1] tai *moss*
苗[2] miao *sprout*
苛[1] ko *vexatious*
苞[1] bao *bud*
苟[3] gou *careless, if*
若[4] roh *if*
苦[3] ku *bitter*
英[1] ying *flower, brave*
茂[4] mao *flourishing*
茄[1] chieh *eggplant*
茅[2] mao *reeds*

six strokes

荔[4] li *li-chi, a fruit*
茫[2] mang *head of grain*
茲[1] dzï *this*
茴[2] hwei *fennel*
茶[2] cha *tea*
荊[1] ging *thorn*
草[3] tsao *grass*
荐[4] dzien *recommend*
荒[1] huang *dearth*

seven strokes

荳[4] dou *bean*
荷[2] ho *lotus*
莊[1] djwang *sedate, farm*
莠[4] yu *weeds*
莫[4] mo *do not*
莽[3] mang *jungle*

eight strokes

菊[1] djüh *chrysanthemum*
菌[4] djwen *mould, bacteria*
菓[3] gwo *fruit*
菖[1] chang *flag, reed*
菜[4] tsai *vegetable*
華[2] hua *glorious*
菱[2] ling *water chestnut*
菲[1] fei *frugal*
萄[2] tao *grape*
菩[2] pu *bodhisatva, idol*
萌[2] meng *budding*
萍[2] ping *duckweed*
萬[4] wan *ten thousand*

nine strokes

落[4] lo *to drop, fall*
葉[4] yeh *a leaf*
著[4] dju *write, manifest*
葛[2] goh *hemp, grass cloth*
葡[2] pu *grape*
董[3] dung *gentry, to direct*

葦 3 wei *reed*
葫 2 hu *gourd*
葬 4 dzang *to bury*
葯 3 yoh *medicine*
葱 1 tsung *onion*
葷 1 hwen *leeks, meat*
蒂 4 di *stem*
蒙 2 meng *obscure, cover*

ten strokes

蒜 4 swan *garlic*
蒲 2 pu *rushes*
蒸 1 djen *to steam*
蒼 1 tsang *azure*
蒿 1 hao *moxa, weeds*
蓄 4 hsüh *collect*
蓆 2 hsih *mat*
蓉 2 yung *hibiscus*
蓋 4 gai *cover*
蓑 1 so *grass raincoat*

eleven strokes

蓮 2 lien *lotus*
蔑 4 mieh *a negative*
蔓 4 man *climbing plant*
蔔 4 bo *turnip*
蔗 1 dje *sugar cane*
蔬 1 su *greens*
蔭 4 yin *shadow*
蔽 4 bi *shade, protect*
蕃 2 fan *exuberant*
蕉 1 dziao *plantain*

twelve strokes

蕩 4 dang *waste, disturb*
蕪 2 wu *water grass*
蕭 1 hsiao *artemisia, desolate*
薄 4 boh *thin, slight*
薑 1 giang *ginger*
薦 4 gien *to introduce*
薪 1 hsin *fuel, salary*

fourteen strokes

薰 1 hsün *perfume, burn*
藉 2 dzih *to avail of*
藍 2 lan *blue*
藏 2 tsang *conceal, hoard*
藐 3 miao *neglect, despise*
藕 3 ou *arrowroot*
藝 4 i *skill, art*
藤 2 teng *rattan*
藥 4 yoh *medicine, drug*
藩 2 fan *a fence*
藪 3 sou *lake, marsh*
藻 3 tsao *pondweed, algae*
蘆 2 lu *reeds*
蘇 1 su *to revive*
蘋 2 pin *duckweed*
蘭 2 lan *orchid*
蘸 4 djan *dip, soak*
蘿 2 lo *dodder, turnip*

141

虎 3 hu *tiger*
虐 4 nioh *tyrannical*
虔 2 chien *pious, devout*
處 4 chu *dwell, place*
虛 1 hsü *empty, humble*
虜 3 lo *captive, seize*
虞 2 yü *anxiety*
號 4 hao *trade mark, shop*
虧 1 kuei *broken, debt, loss*

142

虫 chung *worm, insect*
虹 2 hung *rainbow*
蚊 2 wen *mosquito*

four strokes

蚌 3 bang *oyster*
蚓 3 yin *earth-worm*
蚤 4 dzao *flea*
蚯 1 chiu *earth-worm*
蚱 4 dja *species of locust*
蛀 4 dju *moth-eaten*
蛆 1 chü *maggot*

蛇2 she *snake*

蛋4 dan *egg*

six strokes

蛙1 wa *frog*

蛛2 dju *spider*

蛟1 giao *kind of dragon*

蛾2 o *moth*

蜂1 feng *bee, wasp*

蜈2 wu *centipede*

蜘1 djï *spider*

蜜4 mih *honey*

eight strokes

蜩2 tiao *cicada*

蜻1 dzing *dragon fly*

蝎1 hsieh *scorpion*

蝕2 shïh *eclipse, eat away*

蝗2 hwang *locust*

蝙1 bien *bat*

蝟4 wei *hedgehog*

蝠2 fu *bat*

蝦1 hsia *prawn, shrimp*

蝴2 hu *butterfly*

蝶2 tieh *butterfly*

螃2 pang *crab*

螞3 ma *ant, leech*

螢2 ying *firefly*

螺2 lo *spiral, shell*

蟆2 ma *the frog*

蟒3 mang *large serpent*

蟠2 pan *coil around*

蟬2 chan *cicada*

蟲2 chung *worms, insects*

thirteen strokes

蟹3 hsiai *crab*

蟻3 i *ant*

蠅2 ying *fly*

蠍1 hsieh *scorpion*

蠟1 la *beeswax*

蠣4 li *oyster*

蠢3 chwen *stupid*

蠶2 tsan *silkworm*

蠻2 man *uncivilized*

143

血3 hsüeh *blood*

衇4 meh *arteries, veins*

衊4 mieh *defame, libel*

144

行2 hsing *to walk*

衍3 yen *inundate, amplify*

術4 shuh *method, art*

衖4 hung *lane, alley*

街1 giai *street*

衙2 ya *government office*

衝 chung *push, bump*

衛4 wei *guard, post*

衡2 heng *steelyard*

衢2 chü *thoroughfare*

145

衣1 i *clothes*

表3 biao *outside, manifest*

衫1 shan *shirt*

衰1 shwai *fading, decay*

衷1 djung *mind, sincere*

衾2 chin *quilt*

衿1 gin *lapel*

袁2 yüen *a name*

袂4 mei *sleeve*

袋4 dai *bag, pouch*

袍2 pao *wadded robe*

袖4 hsiu *sleeve*

被4 bei *coverlet*

six strokes

袱4 fuh *wrapper*

袴4 ku *trousers*

裁2 tsai *cut, reduce*

裂2 lieh *split, tear*

裏3 li *inside*

裔4 i *posterity*

裕[4] yü *abundance*
裘[2] chiu *fur garment*
裙[2] chün *skirt, petticoat*
補[3] bu *mend, repair*
裝[1] djuang *dress, pack*
裳[2] shang *skirt*
裸[3] lo *naked*
裹[3] go *wrap up*
製[4] djï *manufacture*
褂[4] gua *jacket*
複[4] fuh *double*
褊[3] bien *narrow, small*

ten strokes

褥[4] ruh *cushion*
褲[4] ku *trousers*
褻[4] hsieh *undress, desecrate*
襄[1] hsiang *finish, assist*
襖[3] ao *short garment*
襟[1] gin *lapel*
襪[4] wa *socks*
襯[4] tsen *inner garment*
襲[4] hsih *inherit, wear*

146

西[1] hsi *west*
要[4] yao *desire, to will*
覆[42] fu *upset, reply*

147

見[4] gien *see*
規[1] gwei *compasses, usage*
覓[4] mi *search, look for*
視[4] shï *see, observe*
覩[3] du *see, witness*
親[1] tsin *parents, love*
覺[4] gioh *perception*
覽[3] lan *look, glance*
觀[1] gwan *look at*

148

角[1] gioh *horn, corner*
觔[1] gin *a catty*
解[3] giai *untie, analyze*
觴[1] shang *goblet*
觸[4] chuh *gore, butt*

149

言[2] yen *speech, words*
訂[4] ding *compare, revise*
訃[4] fu *announcement*
計[4] gi *count, plan*
訊[4] hsün *trial, tidings*
討[3] tao *beg, punish*
訓[4] hsün *instruct, follow*
訕[1] shan *slander*
託[4] toh *entrust to*
記[4] gi *remember, record*
訛[2] o *false, deceive*
訟[4] sung *to accuse*
訣[2] güeh *certainly, decide*
訪[3] fang *inquire, visit*
設[4] sheh *institute, set up*
許[3] hsü *grant, permit*

five strokes

訴[4] su *inform, tell*
註[4] dju *explanation*
証[4] djeng *witness, appeal*
詆[3] di *calumniate*
詈[4] li *abuse, rail at*
詐[4] dja *deceive*
詔[4] djao *announce, proclaim*
評[3] ping *criticise*
詛[3] dzu *curse*
詞[2] tzï *word, phrase*
詠[4] yung *chant*
詢[2] hsün *ask, consult*
試[4] shï *test, verify*
詫[4] dja *artful, amazing*
詭[3] gwei *deceive*
詩[1] shï *poem*
話[4] hwa *word, speech*

該1 gai *ought, to owe*
詳2 tsiang *carefully*
誅1 dju *kill, execute*
誇1 kwa *boast*

seven strokes

誌4 djï *record, history*
認4 ren *know, admit*
誑4 kwang *mislead*
誓4 shï *swear, oath*
誕4 dan *boast, birthday*
誘4 yu *lead on, entice*
語3 yü *words, answer*
誠2 cheng *truth, sincerity*
誡4 giai *warn, order*
誣2 wu *slander*
誤4 wu *mistake*
誥4 gao *order, tell*
誨3 hwei *instruct*
誦4 sung *read, chant*
說4 shoh *speak, explain*

eight strokes

誰2 shui *who?*
課4 ko *lesson, tax*
調4 {diao, *tune*
調2 {tiao, *blend*
諂3 chan *flatter*
談2 tan *converse*
諉3 wei *shirk, implicate*
請3 tsing *invite, engage*
諒4 liang *excuse*
論4 lwen *discourse*
諄1 djwen *enjoin, earnest*
諫4 gien *remonstrate*
諭4 yü *order, analogy*
諱4 hwei *avoid, conceal*
諷1 feng *revile, satirize*
諸1 dju *all, every, upon*
諺4 yen *proverb*
諳4 an *experienced*
謀2 mou *plan, plot*
謁4 yeh *visit*
謂4 wei *tell, say*
謄2 teng *copy*
謎4 mi *riddle*

ten strokes

謔4 hsioh *banter*
謗3 bang *slander*
謙1 chien *humble*
講3 giang *tell, preach*
謝4 hsie *thank, decline*
謠2 yao *ballad, rumour*
謫4 dzeh *blame, fault*
謬4 miu *fallacy*
謨2 mo *to plan, imitate*
謹3 gin *careful*
譁2 hwa *clamour*
證4 djeng *prove, verify*
譏1 gi *to blame, ridicule*
識2 shïh *know, recognise*

thirteen strokes

譜3 pu *genealogy*
譟4 sao *clamour*
警3 ging *warn, arouse*
譬4 pi *comparison*
譯1 ih *translate*
議4 i *discuss*
譴3 chien *reprimand*
護4 hu *save, guard*
譽4 yü *praise*
讀2 duh *read*
變4 bien *change*
讎2 chou *revenge, hate*
讒2 chan *detract*
讓4 rang *waive, yield to*
讚4 dzan *commend, eulogy*
讟2 duh *sedition, slander*

150

谷 guh *a valley*
谿1 chi *stream, brook*
豁1 hwoh *open, intelligent*

151

豆4 dou *bean family*
豈3 chi *interrogative "can it be"*
鼓4 gu *a drum*
登1 deng *ascend*
豎4 shu *to erect*
豐1 feng *abundant*

twenty-one strokes

豔4 yen *beautiful*

152

豕 shï *a pig*
象4 hsiang *an elephant*
豪2 hao *the least*
豫4 yü *to hesitate*
豬1 dju *a pig*

153

豸 djai *reptiles*
豹4 bao *leopard*
豺2 chai *a wolf*
貂1 diao *sable fur*
貌4 mao *appearance*

nine strokes

貓2 mao *a cat*

154

貝4 bei *precious*

two strokes

貞1 djen *chaste, pure*
負4 fu *carry, ungrateful*
財2 tsai *wealth*
貢4 gung *tribute*
貧2 pin *poor*
貨4 ho *goods*
販4 fan *to peddle*
貪1 tan *to covet*
貫4 gwan *to pass through*
責2 dzeh *to rebuke*

five strokes

貯4 dju *to amass*
貳4 er *two*
貴4 gwei *honourable*
貶3 bien *blame*
買3 mai *to buy*
貸4 dai *to lend*
費4 fei *to spend*
貼4 tieh *to adhere*
貽2 i *to transmit*
貿4 mao *to trade*
賀4 ho *to congratulate*
賁1 ben *energetic*

six strokes

賂4 lu *bribery*
賃4 ren *to rent*
賄4 hwei *bribe.*
資1 dzï *wealth*
賈3 { gia, *surname* / gu, *a merchant* }
賊4 dzei *a thief*

seven strokes

賑4 djen *to succour*
賓1 bin *a guest*
賒1 she *to lend, give*
賠2 pei *compensate, lose*
賬4 djang *account, debt*
賜4 tzï *to bestow*
賞3 shang *to reward*
賢2 hsien *worthy*
賣4 mai *to sell*
賤4 gien *cheap*
賦4 fu *to bestow*
質4 djïh *a pledge, substance*

nine strokes

賭3 du *to gamble*
賴4 lai *pretend, rely*
賸4 sheng *surplus*
購4 gou *to purchase*
賽4 sai *to compete*
賺4 djwan *make profit*

eleven strokes

贄4 djïh *a present*
贅4° djui *reiterate*

贈4 dzeng *to give*
贊4 dzan *to praise, assist*
贏2 ying *to win*
贓1 dzang *booty*

fifteen strokes

贖2 shuh *to redeem*

155

赤4 chĭh *red*
赦4 she *to forgive*
赫4 heh *to frighten*

156

走3 dzou *to walk*
赴4 fu *to go*
起3 chi *raise up*
趁4 chen *seize an opportunity*
超1 chao *to exceed*
越4 yüeh *to pass over*
趣4 tsü *pleasure*

ten strokes

趨1 tsü *move toward*

157

足4 dzuh *a foot, enough*
跋4 boh *conclusion*
跌1 dieh *to fall*
跑2 pao *to run*

six strokes

跟1 gen *to follow*
跡4 dzih *trace, results*
跨4 kwa *to stride*
跪4 gwei *to kneel*
路4 lu *a road*
跳4 tiao *to jump*
踏4 tah *to trample*
踐4 gien *to follow*
踝3 hwa *the ankle*

nine strokes

踵3 djung *the heel, to follow*
蹂2 rou *trample on*
蹄2 ti *a hoof*

eleven strokes

蹟4 dzih *a footprint*
蹤1 dzung *follow*
蹲1 tseng *to squat*

158

身1 shen *the body*
躬1 gung *I, myself*
躭1 dan *to desire, lust*
躲3 do *to escape*
躺3 tang *to lie down*

159

車1 che *a cart*
軋4 ya *to crush*
軌3 gwei *rails a track*
軍1 gün *an army*
軛4 eh *a yoke*
軟3 rwan *soft, feeble*
軸2 djou *an axle*
較3 giao *to compare*
載3 dzai *to load*
輕1 ching *light*

eight strokes

輝1 hwei *brilliance*
輦3 nien *imperial chariot*
輩4 bei *class, generation*
輪2 lwen *a wheel*

nine strokes

輭 rwan *weak*
輸1 shu *to lose*
輾3 djan *to turn*
轂1 guh *the hub*
轄2 hsiah *to govern*
轆4 luh *to revolve*
轉3 djwan *to turn*

thirteen strokes

轎4 giao *a sedan chair*
轟1 hung *to rumble*

160

辛 hsin *bitter*
辜1 gu *transgression, calamity*

six strokes

辠4 dzui *sin*
辦4 ban *to manage*
辨4 bien *to distinguish, argue*

thirteen strokes

辭2 tzï *to dismiss*
辯4 bien *discuss, argue*

161

辰3 chen *an hour*
辱3 ruh *insult, defile*

six strokes

農2 neng *farmer, agriculture*

162

辵 djoh *walking*
迂1 yü *distant, vague*
迄4 chih *until, reach to*
迅4 hsün *sudden, quick*
迎2 ying *receive, welcome*
近4 gin *near*
返3 fan *to return*

five strokes

迥3 giung *far from*
迦1 gia *Buddhist sound*
迪2 dih *to lead*
迫4 peh *to press, urge*
迭2 dieh *to alternate*
述4 shuh *to relate*

six strokes

迴2 hwei *to revolve*
迷2 mi *wandered, deceived*
迹4 dzih *a trace*
迺3 nai *but, nevertheless*
追1 djui *to pursue*
退4 tui *retreat, push back*
送4 sung *to present*
逃2 tao *to escape*
逆4 nih *oppose*

seven strokes

逢2 feng *to meet, appoint*
逍1 hsiao *easy, to stroll*
逐2 djuh *expel, seriatim*
透4 tou *to permeate*
逑2 chiu *seek, unite*
途2 tu *a road*
逕4 ging *a path*
通1 tung *thoroughfare*
逝4 shï *pass away*
逞3 cheng *presumptuous*
速4 suh *quickly*
這4 dje *this*
造4 dzao *to create*
連2 lien *connected*

eight strokes

逮4 dai *to reach to*
進4 dzin *to enter*
逸4 ih *to retire, excess*
逼4 bih *compel*
逾2 yü *pass over*
遁4 dun *escape, hide*
遂4 sui *accord with*
遍4 bien *everywhere*
過4 go *transgress*
遏4 oh *oppose, hinder*
遐2 hsia *distant*
道4 dao *the way, reason*
運4 yün *revolve, fortune*
遊2 yu *to travel*
遇4 yü *to meet*
達2 dah *reach to*
違2 wei *opposed*

ten strokes

遙2 yao *remote*
遛2 liu *to saunter*
遜4 swen *yield, recede*
遞4 di *to hand to*
遡4 su *go up, push*
遠3 yüen *distant*
遣3 chien *to send*

eleven strokes

適4 shïh *now, suddenly*
遭1 dzao *to meet*

遮 1 dje *to screen*
遲 2 chī *slow, late*

twelve strokes

遵 1 dzwen *follow, obey*
遶 3 rao *circuitous*
遷 1 tsien *to remove*
選 3 hsüen *to choose*
遺 2 i *to transmit*

thirteen strokes

遽 4 gü *hurriedly*
避 4 bi *to escape, avoid*
邀 1 yao *ramble*
邁 4 mai *aged*
還 2 hwan *to return, repay*
邇 3 er *near*
邊 1 bien *the side*

163

邑 ih *a region*
那 3 na *that, where?*
邦 1 bang *place, country*
邪 2 hsie *depraved*
郊 1 giao *suburbs*
郎 2 lang *a gentleman*
郡 4 gün *a district*
郤 4 chioh *but, still*

eight strokes

部 4 bu *section*
郭 1 gwoh *edge, outside*
郵 2 yu *post office*
都 1 du *capital, all*
鄉 1 hsiang *rural, country*
鄙 4 bi *rustic, rude*
鄧 4 deng *steps*

twelve strokes

鄰 2 lin *neighbouring*

164

酉 3 yu *5-7 p.m.*
酋 2 dziu *chieftain*
酌 1 djoh *arrange, discuss*
配 4 pei *to mate, match*
酒 3 dziu *wine, spirits*
酣 1 han *drunk*
酥 1 su *soft, curds*

six strokes

酬 2 chou *return favour*
酵 4 giao *leaven*
酷 4 kuh *cruel*
酸 1 swan *sour*
醃 1 yen *to pickle*
醇 2 chwen *strong, thick*
醉 4 dzui *drunk*
醋 4 tsu *vinegar*

nine strokes

醒 1 hsing *to awake*
醜 3 chou *ugly, nasty*
醫 1 i *to heal*
醬 4 dziang *soy, ketchup*
醲 2 neng *good wine*
釀 4 nang *to brew, provoke*
釁 4 hsin *stir up strife*

165

釆 bien *distinguish*
釋 5 shīh *to explain*

166

里 3 li *a mile*
重 4 djung *heavy*
野 3 ye *wild, wilderness*
量 2 liang *to measure*
釐 2 li *a thousandth part, a tax, likin*

167

金 1 gin *metal, gold*
釘 1 ding *a nail*
釜 3 fu *a cauldron*
針 1 djen *a needle*
釣 4 diao *a hook*
鈕 4 kou *a button*
釵 1 chai *a hairpin*

four strokes

鈍 4 dun *blunt*

鈎1 gou *a hook*
鈔1 chao *money, coin*
鈕3 niu *a button*
鈞1 gün *heavy, great*
鈴2 ling *a bell*

five strokes

鈸4 boh *cymbals, bowl*
鉢4 boh *begging bowl*
鉛1 chien *lead*
鉋4 bao *plane, to plane*
銀2 yin *silver*
銅2 tung *brass*
銜2 hsien *a gag, rank*

seven strokes

鋭4 rui *sharp, keen*
銷1 hsiao *expend, dissipate*
銼4 tso *a file*
鋒1 feng *the point, first*
鋤2 chu *a spade*
鋪1 pu *to spread, pave*

eight strokes

鋸4 gü *a saw*
鋼1 gang *steel*
錄4 luh *record, emolument*
錐1 djui *an awl*
錘2 chui *a hammer*
錠4 ding *ingot of silver*
錢2 tsien *money*
錦3 gin *embroidery*
錫1 hsih *pewter*
錯4 tso *a mistake, error*

nine strokes

鍊4 lien *to refine*
鍋1 go *a pot*
鍍4 du *to enamel*
鍛4 dwan *to smelt*
錨2 mao *anchor*
鍵3 lien *tongue of lock*
鍼1 djen *a needle*

ten strokes

鎖3 so *a lock*
鎗1 chiang *a spear*
鎚2 chui *a mallet*
鎮4 djen *subject, a market*
鏇2 hsüen *a lathe*
鏟3 chan *a shovel*
鏡4 ging *a mirror*
鏈4 lien *chain*

twelve strokes

鐘1 djung *a bell, clock*
鐮2 lien *a scythe*
鐲3 djoh *a bracelet*
鐵3 tieh *iron*
鐶2 hwan *ring, ear-ring,*
鐸2 doh *a bell*
鑄4 dju *mould, cast*
鑑4 gien *examine*
鑰4 yoh *a key*
鑼2 lo *a gong*
鑽1 dzwan *a drill, to bore*
鑿2 dzoh *to pierce, sink a well*

168

長3 djang, *elder*
長2 chang, *long*

169

門2 men *a door*
閂1 shwan *to bar*
閃3 shan *to flash*
閉4 bi *to close*
開1 kai *to open*
閑2 hsien *leisure, hinder*
閒2 hsien, *idle, unhurried*
間 gien *between, a room*
閔3 min *to feel for*

five strokes

閏4 rwen *intercalary month*
閣2 goh *council chamber*
閤2 hoh *the whole family*
閨1 gwei *female apartments*

閹 1 yen *to castrate*
閻 2 yen *village gate*

nine strokes

闊 4 kwoh *wide, spacious*
闔 2 hoh *whole, a door*
闖 [illegible] chwang *rude, dash*
關 1 gwan *a gate, pass*
闢 4 pih *to open, split*

170

阜 fou *a mound*
防 2 fang *a bank, guard*
阻 3 dzu *to hinder*
阿 1 a *final particle*
陀 2 to *a declivity*
附 4 fu *near, to join*

six strokes

陋 4 lou *rustic*
降 4 giang *to descend*
限 4 hsien *a limit*
陛 4 bi *steps of the throne*
陞 1 sheng *be promoted*
陡 3 dou *steep*
院 4 yüen *courtyard*
陣 4 djen *army, repeated*
除 2 chu *except*

eight strokes

陪 2 pei *accompany, reply*
陳 2 chen *stale, a name*
陵 2 ling *a tomb*
陶 2 tao *a potter*
陰 1 yin *dark, female principle*
陷 4 hsien *fall into*
陸 4 luh *six, land*

nine strokes

陽 2 yang *light, male principle*
隄 2 di *a bank*
隆 2 lung *abundant*
隊 4 dui *army, troop*
階 1 giai *steps*
隔 1 geh *separated*

thirteen strokes

隣 2 lin *neighbouring*
遂 4 sui *follow, there-upon*
隨 2 sui *follow*
險 3 hsien *dangerous*
隱 3 wen *firm*

171

隶 wei *tanned hide*
隸 4 li *to control*

172

隹 djui *birds*
隻 1 djï *one thing*
雀 3 chioh *a bird*
雁 4 yen *wild goose*
雄 2 hsiung *male, hero*
雅 3 ya *elegant*
集 2 dzih *to collect*
雇 4 gu *to hire*

five strokes

雌 1 tzï *female*
雍 1 yung *harmonious*
雕 1 diao *to engrave*
雖 1 sui *although*

ten strokes

雙 1 shwang *a pair*
雛 2 gü *young birds*
雜 2 dzah *mixed*
雞 1 gi *hen, chicken*
離 2 li *leave, go away*
難 2 nan *difficulty*

173

雨 3 yü *rain*
雪 4 hsüeh *snow*
雲 2 yün *clouds*
零 2 ling *fragmentary*
雷 2 lei *thunder*
雹 2 {bao, boh *hailstones*

L.

電4 dien *lightning*

six strokes

需1 hsü *necessary*
霄1 hsiao *the sky*
震4 djen *to rumble, shake*
霖2 lin *dripping*
霜1 shwang *frost*
霞2 hsia *variegated*

eleven strokes

霧4 wu *mist*
霪2 yin *disastrous rain*
露4 { lou, *dew* / lu }
霸4 ba *despotism*
靈2 ling *spiritual*

174

青1 ching *sky-blue*
靛4 dien *indigo*
靜4 dzing *quiet, clear*

175

非1 fei *negative*
靠4 kao *lean, depend*
靡3 mi *to waste*

176

面4 mien *face*

177

革2 goh *leather*
靴1 hsüe *top boots*
靶3 ba *a target*
鞋2 hsiai *shoes*
鞍1 an *saddle*
鞏3 gung *secure*

seven strokes

鞘1 hsiao *a scabbard*
鞦1 chiu *a swing*
鞭1 bien *a whip*

178

韋 wei *tanned hide*
韓2 han *a name*
韜1 tao *military art*

179

韭3 djiu *leeks*

180

音1 yin *sound*
韻4 yün *riming tone*
響3 hsiang *noise, sound*

181

頁4 yeh *a leaf*
頂3 ding *tip, extremely*
頃3 ching *a moment*
項4 hsiang *the neck*
順4 shwen *obey, favourable*
須1 hsü *necessary*

four strokes

頌4 sung *to praise*
預4 yü *prepare*
頑2 wan *stubborn, evil*
頒1 ban *to proclaim*
頓4 dwen *a time, a meal*
頗3 po *very*
領3 ling *a collar, leader*
頭2 tou *the head*
頰1 giah *the jaws*
頸3 ging *the neck*
頹2 tui *ruined*
顆3 ko *a grain, bead*
顋1 sai *cheeks*
題2 ti *a theme, text*
額2 eh *forehead, a number*
顏2 yen *colour*

ten strokes

願4 yüen *willing, wish*
顙3 sang *forehead*
顛1 dien *inverted*
類4 lui *kind, class*
顧4 gu *look upon*
顫4 chan *to tremble*
顯3 hsien *to manifest*

182

風[1] feng *wind*
颳[1] gwa *to blow*
颺[2] yang *spread abroad*
飄[1] piao *a whirlwind*

183

飛[1] fei *fly*

184

食[2] shïh *food*
飢[1] gi *hungry*
飩[2] tun *a meal*
飲[3] yin *to drink*
飯[4] fan *food*
飼[4] szï *to feed*
飽[3] bao *satisfied*
飾[4] shïh *adornment*

six strokes

餉[4] hsiang *rations*
養[3] yang *to nourish*
餌[4] er *bait*
餐[1] tsan *a meal*
餑[1] boh *a dumpling*
餓[4] o *hunger*
餘[2] yü *abundance*

eight strokes

餚[2] hsiao *delicacies*
餞[3] gien *comfits*
餅[3] bing *cake, biscuit*
餧[4] wei *feed animals*
館[3] gwan *lodging, inn*
餬[2] hu *sustenance*

ten strokes

餻[1] gao *cakes, dumplings*
餽[4] kwei *present of food*
饅[2] man *bread*
饋[4] kuei *food*
饌[4] djwan *to nourish*
饑[1] gi *hunger*
饒[2] rao *abundant, forgive*
饕[1] tao *greedy, covetous*
饗[3] hsiang *sacrifice, a meal*

fourteen strokes

饜[4] yen *satiated*

185

首[3] shou *head*

186

香[1] hsiang *incense*
馥[4] fuh *fragrance*
馨[1] hsing *incense, merit*

187

馬[3] ma *horse*
馭[4] yü *control*
馱[2] toh *to carry*
馳[2] chï *to gallop, swiftly*
馴[2] hsün *docile, tame*
駁[2] boh *to confute, argue*

five strokes

駐[4] dju *halting place*
駒[1] gü *a colt*
駕[4] gia *a carriage*
駙[4] fu *follow, close to*
駛[3] shï *to guide*
駝[2] to *a camel*
駟[4] szï *four horse chariot*
駭[3] hsieh *startled*
騃[3] ai *stupid*

eight strokes

騎[2] chi *to ride*
騙[4] pien *swindle*
騰[2] teng *to rise, compete, race*
騷[1] sao *sad, annoy*
騾[2] lo *a mule*
驁[2] ao *stubborn*
驅[1] chü *expel*
驕[1] giao *proud, restive*
驗[4] yen *verify, inspect*
驚[1] ging *startled*

驛4 ih *a post-house*
驢2 lü *a donkey*

188

骨2 guh *a bone*
骰3 shai *dice*
骷1 ku *a skeleton*
骸2 hai *skeleton*
髏2 lou *skull*
髑2 duh *a skull*
髒1 dzang *dirty*
髓3 sui *marrow*
體3 ti *the body*

189

高1 gao *high*

190

髟 biao *shaggy*
髮3 fah *hair*
髯2 ran *beard*
髻4 gih *tufts of hair*
鬆1 sung *loose*
鬍2 hu *beard*
鬚1 hsü *moustache*

191

鬥 dou *fight*
鬧4 nao *to quarrel*
鬨4 hung *be rowdy*
鬭4 dou *fight*
鬮1 giu *lots, ballot*

192

鬯 chang *sacrificial bowl*
鬱4 yüh *pent up sorrow*

193

鬲 goh *sacrificial vase*
鬻4 yüh *to sell*

194

鬼3 gwei *demon*
魁1 kwei *gigantic*
魂2 hwen *soul*
魄4 poh *earthly soul*
魅4 mei *sprite*
魎3 liang *ghost*
魏4 wei *ancient State*
魑1 chï *brownie*
魔2 mo *devil*

195

魚2 yü *fish*
魯3 lu *ancient State*
鮮1 hsien *fresh*
鯉3 li *a carp*
鯊1 sha *a shark*
鯨2 ging *whale*
鰉2 鱑 hwang *eel*
鰕1 hsia *shrimp*
鰥1 gwan *widower*

eleven strokes

鰲2 ao *monster*
鱉1 bieh *the turtle*
鱗2 lin *scales*
鱷4 鰐 oh *crocodile*

196

鳥3 niao *bird*
鳧2 fu *wild duck*
鳩1 giu *pigeon*
鳲 shï *the cuckoo*
鳳4 feng *the phoenix*
鳴2 ming *to call*
鳶1 yüen *a kite*

four strokes

鴇3 bao *bustard*
鴈4 yen *wild goose*
鴉1 ya *the rook*
鴛1 yüen *Mandarin drake*
鴞1 hsiao *an owl*
鴟1 chï *an owl*

鴣 1 gu *the partridge*
鴦 1 yang *Mandarin duck*
鴨 1 ya *a duck*

six strokes

鴻 2 hung *great, vast*
鴿 1 goh *a dove*
鵝 2 o *the goose*
鵡 3 wu *parrot*
鵬 2 peng *the roc*
鵲 3 chioh *birds*
鶉 2 chun *quail*
鵪 an *a quail*
鶴 2 hoh *crane*

ten strokes

鷄 1 gi *the hen*
鷹 1 ying *eagle*
鷺 1 lu *egret, heron*
鸚 1 ying *parrot*
鸝 1 li *oriole*

197

鹵 3 lu *natural salt*
鹹 2 hsien *salty*
鹽 2 yen *salt*

198

鹿 luh *a deer*
麒 2 chi *a unicorn*
麝 4 she *musk deer*
麟 2 lin *unicorn*
麤 1 tsu *coarse*

199

麥 4 meh *wheat*
麩 1 fu *bran*
麪 4 mien *flour*
麴 1 chü *leaven*

200

麻 2 ma *hemp*
麽 2 {ma, mo} *interrogative*

201

黃 2 hwang *yellow*

202

黍 shu *millet*
黎 2 li *black hair*
黏 2 nien *glutinous*

203

黑 heh *black*
黔 2 chien *black*
默 4 meh *silent*
黛 4 dai *a black gem*
黜 1 chuh *degrade, dismiss*
點 3 dien *a dot*
黨 3 dang *a clique*

204

黹 djih *embroidery*
黻 4 fuh } *embroidered robe*
黼 3 fu }

205

黽 min *a frog*
黿 2 yüen *sea monster*
鼇 2 ao *a big fish*
鼈 1 bieh *sea turtle*

206

鼎 ding *tripod*
鼐 4 nai *incense tripod*

207

鼓 3 gu *a drum*
鼕 1 dung *roll of drums*

208

鼠 shu *a rat*

209

鼻 2 bi *the nose*
鼾 1 han *snore*

210

齊 2 chi *even*
齋 1 djai *abstain from meat*

211

齒 chï *teeth*
齡[2] ling *teeth, age*
齧[2] nieh *to gnaw*
齩[3] yao *to bite*
齪[4] choh *filthy*
齷[4] woh *filthy*
齟[3] dzu *misunderstand-ing*
齬[3] yü *mistake*

212

龍 lung *dragon*
龐[2] pang *lofty house*
龔[1] gung *a name*
龕[1] kan *a niche*

213

龜[1] guei *tortoise*

214

龠[4] yoh *flute*

NOTE.

It is assumed that the student who proposes to use the dictionary has read pages 18-20 of the Preface and studied the table of radicals, pages 21-29. If so, the method of using the dictionary will be clear to him without further instruction.

For the lessons in the book the dictionary is not necessary, but the student who has worked through the grammar will wish to go on to read some Chinese book and for this will need the dictionary.

The ordinary Chinese-English dictionary contains many characters that the average student never needs to use. Giles's Chinese-English Dictionary contains over 10,000 separate characters, but the Old Testament in Chinese only contains 3,946; the New Testament has 2,713, and this dictionary 3,000.

To the multiplicity of uncommon characters the ordinary dictionary adds under each character numerous and sometimes apparently contradictory meanings which still further confuse the beginner. This dictionary contains no character not in common use, and gives only the principal meaning of each character from which the cognate meanings, if there are any, may be easily deduced. It is anticipated that these features of simplicity and directness will add much to the value of the dictionary.